I ONCE WAS BLIND BUT NOW I SQUINT

Kent Crockett

FOREWORD BY DENNIS SWANBERG

I ONCE WAS BLIND BUT NOW I SQUINT

HOW PERSPECTIVE AFFECTS OUR BEHAVIOR

KENT CROCKETT

Advancing the Ministries of the Gospel
AMG Publishers

God's Word to you is our highest calling.

First printing—January 2004
Cover designed by ImageWright, Inc., Chattanooga, Tennessee
Interior design and typesetting by Reider Publishing Services,
     West Hollywood, California
Edited and Proofread by Jonathan Wright, Dan Penwell, Sharon Neal,
     and Warren Baker

Printed in the United States of America
10 09 08 07 06 05 04 –EB– 8 7 6 5 4 3 2 1

To my children,
Hannah and Scott

Contents

Acknowledgments

I WOULD LIKE to express my gratitude to the following:

My Lord Jesus Christ, who opened my blind eyes and continues to teach me how to view life correctly.

My wife, Cindy; Cathy Evans; and Alesa Meschberger for critiquing my rough drafts.

Pat Howard, Heath Howard, and the Paraclete Group for maintaining my website at www.kentcrockett.com.

David Smith, president, and Jay Orr, vice president, of Brewton-Parker College, Mt. Vernon, Georgia, for furthering God's kingdom through Christian education.

Debbie Cenatiempo for faithfully interceding for me and my ministry.

Dan Penwell and the entire AMG Publishers family for making this book a reality.

Jonathan Wright who did a superb job of editing. I appreciate all you did.

Foreword

By Dennis Swanberg

WHEN I WAS in graduate school, my eye doctor told me
that I was nearsighted. I could easily see things up close
but struggled seeing things far away. My local church leaders
felt the opposite. They said I could see things far away (I was
"Swan the Visionary"), but I wasn't good at seeing the practi-
cal things up close. Who can you please these days?

Anyway . . . whether your sight is 20/20, nearsighted, far-
sighted, or plagued with astigmatism, you need to get the
right perspective. And that's what Kent Crockett has provided in this book.

Everyone has a different point of view. Some perspectives
match with ours—others clash. We must face the fact that we are
reluctant to change our outlooks, even when the facts are clearly
presented. Why? Because we're accustomed to seeing things only
from our own selfish perspectives. Whatever we perceive to be
true, we fight to the death to prove that it is the truth, the
whole truth, and nothing but the truth. At best we only squint!

Yes, it takes a little effort (and humility) to pull back and admit we've been wrong in our perception. But if we do, we'll be able to see things much more clearly, which will keep us from stumbling.

I like this book! I like the spirit and heart of Kent Crockett! You can tell by every paragraph that he's "living it" with us. He's been there and done that, but he's still making adjustments in the way he looks at things. We all need to have a spiritual eye checkup from time to time. We would do well to take heed from Kent in the matter of perspective.

So go get a cup of coffee or a diet drink, find your favorite chair, and have a good read. And most of all—enjoy discovering a new perspective on life!

Dr. Dennis Swanberg
America's Minister of Encouragement/
Author/TV Host/Speaker/Entertainer

PART 1

Forming Your Perspective

> **Perspective: a specific point of view in understanding people, things, or events**

If you could win an Olympic medal, which would you prefer—the silver or the bronze?

A study of Olympic medal winners produced some unexpected results. Most people would assume the silver medal winners would be happier than the bronze medalists since they received a higher honor, but that wasn't the case. The bronze medalists, who came in third place, were found to be happier than the silver medalists, who finished in second place.

The former Olympians explained how they felt about their medals. The third-place winners were thrilled just to have won a medal. The silver medalists, on the other hand, felt like losers because they didn't come in first place.[1]

Don't read any further until you grasp this astounding truth: What happens to you is not nearly as important as *how you perceive what happens to you.*

ONE

In the Eye of the Beholder

We view things not only from different sides but with different eyes.

~BLAISE PASCAL

IN AN EPISODE of the popular "Peanuts" comic strip series, Charlie Brown, Linus, and Lucy are lying on a hillside looking up at the clouds.

"If you use your imagination you can see lots of things in the cloud formations. What do you see, Linus?" Lucy asks.

"Well, those clouds up there look like a map of the British Honduras on the Caribbean. That cloud up there looks a little like the profile of Thomas Eakins, a famous painter. And that group of clouds over there gives me the impressions of the stoning of Stephen. I can see the apostle Paul standing there to one side," Linus replies.

"What do *you* see in the clouds, Charlie Brown?" Lucy inquires.

"Well, I was going to say I saw a ducky and a horsey—but I changed my mind."

Just as we can see different things when we look at clouds, we can also see different things when we view life. Pastor Ed Manning tells about a situation when a woman approached him to ask a question. As she drew closer to him, he tipped his head back to look through the bottom lenses of his bifocals to focus on her more clearly.

"There you go again!" the woman exploded. "You stick your nose up in the air every time I talk to you! Who do you think you are? I'm sick of your arrogant attitude!"

Pastor Manning was taken aback by her outburst of anger.

"You don't understand," he explained. "I'm not sticking my nose up in the air at you. I just can't see you when you get near me. I'm tilting my head back so I can see you through the bottom half of my bifocals."

The woman had misperceived the situation. She had been harboring resentment toward him, thinking he had been looking down at her. Although it wasn't true, that's how she viewed their relationship. Pastor Manning wore bifocals, but she wore *rejection glasses.*

She's not alone. The world is filled with people who misinterpret what they see. It's been a problem since biblical times.

King Saul acquired a perverted perspective on the day he heard Israeli women praising David's accomplishments more than his own. Through *jealousy glasses* he "looked at David with suspicion from that day on" (1 Sam. 18:6–9). Ten spies sneaked into the land of Canaan, looked through *inferiority glasses* and said, "We became like grasshoppers in our own sight, and so we were in their sight" (Num. 13:33). The vineyard workers looked through *envy glasses,* compared dollars per hour, and griped about their paychecks (see Matt. 20:10–16). The Pharisees viewed Jesus through *judgmental glasses,* trying to find fault with the perfect Son of God (see Luke 6:7).

Perspective is in the eye of the beholder. Rejection, jealousy, and inferiority are just a few of the attitudes that create

logjams in a viewer's eyes. We
all perceive the world in our
own unique way. Everyone
views and interprets life differently, even when our eyes are
fixed on the same thing.

**Perspective is in the
eye of the beholder.**

Many of the problems we
have with each other are cre-
ated because of our mismatched perspectives. A movie
reviewer assigns a four-star rating to a film while another critic
gives it only one star. And they both watched the same movie.

How many times have we clashed with someone because
we didn't see eye to eye? Husbands and wives quarrel with each
other because they view issues differently. Employees don't get
along with bosses because of their opposing perspectives.
Politicians debate the same issues with contrary opinions.

Why do people see things so differently?

Very simple. It's the glasses we wear.

But these are special glasses; they're not worn on our eyes.
These glasses are worn on our heart. They're devilish lenses
that distort the way we view life.

Satan hands his demons a work order for the destruction
he wants to accomplish each day. Hell's workshop is laboring
overtime, making glasses so we'll see our world in twisted, perverted ways. The enemy knows that if he can distort our perspectives, we'll respond with wrong attitudes and actions. A
warped outlook on life will cause us to sink into depression,
withdraw from relationships, view others suspiciously, and even
hate ourselves. Many of us live in defeat because we look at life
through the devil's glasses instead of through God's eyes.

∾ The Eyes Have It

Perspective is created when our eyes and hearts exchange
information. Although we see with our eyes, we perceive with

our hearts (see John 12:40). Perception is the way our hearts interpret what we see. The attitude that fills our hearts forms the glasses through which we view our world.

We don't see things alike because we don't wear the same glasses. Suppose three people are seated in a room, each wearing various colored sunglasses. Each person looks at the same white piece of paper lying on the table. The one wearing pink glasses sees the paper as pink; the person with yellow glasses views yellow; and the one wearing blue glasses sees blue. When asked to explain what they see, they argue about the true color of the paper.

They each view the paper as a different color because they look through different glasses. Each claims to be right, but none see it correctly. Their colored lenses filter the way they perceive the paper, so they can't see it as white.

> We see things differently because of the glasses we wear.

The same principle applies to the way we view life. Wrong attitudes color our perspectives, so we see things in tainted ways. Until we take off our glasses, we can't see things as they really are. We're merely fooling ourselves into thinking we see correctly.

The different kinds of spectacles are as many as the attitudes that contaminate our hearts. Negative people view their world through *pessimist glasses*. Restless people constantly search for greener grass because they look through *discontentment glasses*. People who imagine that others avoid them wear *rejection glasses*. *Inferiority glasses* make people see themselves in a self-destructive way. Looking through *envy glasses* makes viewers upset when others appear to have more.

When these attitudes seize control of our hearts, our perspective gets thrown out of whack. We see things from a twisted point of view which affects the way we act and react.

Perspective affects *our moods*. The way we perceive things can lift us to the highest state of ecstasy or it can plunge us into the lowest pit of depression.

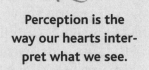

Perception is the way our hearts interpret what we see.

Perspective affects *our relationships*. We assume what others are thinking, even though it may not be true. Our perception creates conflict and confusion in the way we relate to one another.

Perspective affects *our decisions*. We can imagine the most unlikely scenarios and react unwisely.

Can you see how perspectives control how we think and what we do? If we perceive wrongly, we can suddenly find ourselves in trouble. Is there any way to fix the perspective problem?

If You Were Married to You

I'm sure you think that if everyone could look through your eyes, the world's problems would be solved. There would finally be peace on earth and good will toward men.

OK—your wish is granted.

Let's suppose that everyone on this planet is an absolutely identical clone of you. You all have the same preferences and opinions. Everyone thinks the same. Each individual sees from your viewpoint.

Now imagine—hypothetically, of course—that *you* are married to *you*. Would you have a perfect marriage? Would you ever argue with yourself? What if you both wanted the last piece of chicken? Suppose neither of you wanted to take out the trash. What if you were both in bad moods?

Yes, you would still have arguments with yourself if you were married to you. You would find out how difficult it can be to live with yourself. You might even ask yourself for a divorce!

> If *you* were married to *you*, you might want a divorce.

If everyone in the world had identical perspectives, we would still have conflicts. Why? Because we're all selfish. Self insists on seeing everything through its own dogmatic point of view. "All the ways of a man are clean in his own sight, but the Lord weighs the motives" (Prov. 16:2).

This is why we look at things so differently. We're self-centered in our own peculiar ways. We're looking through sin-stained, selfish glasses which tarnish the way we view our world. These tinted lenses on our hearts pervert our perspectives and prevent us from seeing things as they really are. Ungodly attitudes pollute our hearts, which creates distortion in our vision.

We look at circumstances from a human point of view.

We behold others through judgmental eyes.

We see ourselves in comparison to others.

King Solomon tells us, "Do not be wise in your own eyes; fear the Lord and turn away from evil" (Prov. 3:7). Taking off our glasses and focusing on the right things can correct our vision.

We can look at our circumstances from His heavenly viewpoint.

We can behold others through His compassionate eyes.

We can see ourselves as His marvelous handiwork.

Perspective can be corrected, but it begins with a change of heart.

TWO

The Heart of the Problem

We don't see things as they are; we see them as we are.

~ANAIS NIN

I T READS LIKE a page borrowed from *Ripley's Believe It or Not*. When some transplant patients received their new hearts, they discovered that the previous owners had donated a few eerie thoughts as well—just to make it interesting. After recovering from their operation, several recipients started recounting incidents that occurred in their donors' lives.

- A fifty-two-year-old man loved classical music, but after being given the heart of a teenage boy, suddenly discovered that he loved rock music.
- After an eight-year-old girl received the heart of a murdered child, she started having recurring nightmares. She described the circumstances of her donor's death and the killer in such detail that the police were able to capture the murderer, who was later convicted.

- A man suddenly became prone to bouts of depression after his heart transplant. He didn't know that his donor had been a young woman who had been fighting depression.
- A man who received a heart from a woman who was hit by a train had recurrent dreams about train wrecks.
- After a young man received his heart transplant, he awoke and told his mother that "everything is copasetic." He had never used that phrase before but later learned that the donor and his wife used it to reassure each other after they had an argument.[1]

New evidence establishes the fact that we think and remember not only with our minds but also with our hearts. *The American Journal of Cardiology* reports the heart has its own mind—a network of neurons, identical to the neural networks in our brains.[2]

A natural explanation, not a supernatural one, solves the mystery of the thoughts inherited by heart transplant recipients. The heart transmits electrical signals that shape the way the brain thinks.[3] These heart transplant patients could recall what their donors had been thinking because the contributors' hearts remembered their thoughts. Scary thought isn't it? If your heart were transplanted into someone else's body, would you want the recipient to know what you had been thinking?

A cartoon depicted a teacher asking her class, "Who knows what evil lurks in the hearts of men?" A student sat at his desk with a guilty look on his face. On the wall behind him, his shadow raised its hand to answer the question!

> What lurks inside our hearts can be downright creepy.

What lurks inside our hearts can be downright creepy. Jesus informed us that without God's intervention, our hearts can produce some pretty horrendous thoughts. He said, "Out of the heart come evil thoughts, murders, adulteries, fornications, thefts, false witness, slanders" (Matt. 15:19). I'll bet you didn't know that all those critters could be prowling around in your heart. Every one of those attitudes will manifest itself through corresponding behavior.

∿ A Mind of Its Own

It took scientists two thousand years to figure out what Jesus told us long ago—that our hearts do actually think. He informed us that evil thoughts proceed from our hearts. The Bible records several incidents in which Jesus knew what people were thinking in their hearts.

> They brought to Him a paralytic lying on a bed. Seeing their faith, Jesus said to the paralytic, "Take courage, son; your sins are forgiven." And some of the scribes said to themselves, "This fellow blasphemes." And Jesus knowing their thoughts said, "Why are you thinking evil in your hearts?" (Matt. 9:2–4).

Jesus heard evil thoughts whispering inside their hearts.

On another occasion, the disciples argued about which one of them was the greatest. Although they probably wanted to keep this a private squabble, Jesus already knew the evil thoughts that lurked within them. Their hearts got into a shouting match with each other, and Jesus heard every word of the debate.

Jesus, knowing what they were thinking in their hearts, took a child and stood him by His side, and said to them, "Whoever receives this child in My name receives Me, and whoever receives Me receives Him who sent Me; for the one who is least among all of you, this is the one who is great" (Luke 9:47, 48).

Other verses confirm the fact that our hearts have a mind of their own. Simeon told Mary, "A sword will pierce even your own soul—to the end that thoughts from many hearts may be revealed" (Luke 2:35). Hebrews 4:12 tells us that the Word of God is "able to judge the thoughts and intentions of the heart." Solomon penned these words: "As he thinketh in his heart, so is he" (Prov. 23:7, KJV). God will judge and "disclose the motives of men's hearts" (1 Cor. 4:5).

And therein lies the problem. It's not *that* we think in our hearts, but *what* we think in our hearts. The heart of the problem is the problem of the heart. "The heart is more deceitful than all else and is desperately sick. Who can understand it?" (Jer. 17:9). The thoughts in our hearts express themselves through words and behavior, not to mention the way we view others.

∼ Candid Camera

Years ago my wife and I recorded many of our family highlights using an 8mm home movie camera. We collected years of precious memories on numerous spools of film, which became antiquated after the invention of video cameras. Some friends living in another state offered to combine all our films onto one videotape. We gladly accepted their generous offer and sent them our films.

Our friends placed an 8mm home movie camera in their living room to project our movies. They also set up a VHS video camera pointed at the screen and recorded the films while the other camera's reels turned. They sent the completed videotape to us.

Cindy and I were anxious to watch the tape of our old movies. We brought out the popcorn and inserted the video into our VCR. But that's where the fun stopped. As we beheld our old home movie films on videotape, we also listened to our friends' remarks. They hadn't realized that when they recorded our films, the video camera also taped their critical comments about us!

When the videotape began, they started making fun of us. As the film continued to roll, their comments turned vicious. With every new scene came a cutting remark or hurtful joke. Daggers entered my heart as I listened to what our friends honestly thought about us. My wife was devastated.

Our friends looked at us through *judgmental glasses*. Although they were cordial to our faces, the video recorded the true thoughts of their hearts.

Who knows what evil lurks in the hearts of men?

God does. Evil thoughts, slander, murder, adultery, and theft are just a few of the destructive attitudes that emerge from the heart (see Matt. 15:19). Thoughts always precede actions. People who commit immoral deeds have been thinking about those sins in their hearts. A murderer thinks about killing before committing the act. Every thief thinks about stealing before performing the deed.

Our heart is the control panel of our being, pushing buttons and pulling levers, which directs our thoughts and actions. "Watch over your heart with all diligence, for from it flow the springs of life" (Prov. 4:23). Your heart dictates not only what your body does but also what your eyes see.

> **Your eyes and heart function together to form your perspective.**

◯ The Eyes of Our Heart

Several factors can influence our perspective, such as the way we were brought up, what we've been taught in school, and our religious, economic, and social backgrounds. Although these affect the way we view life, our heart takes precedence over all factors.

Paul prayed that "the eyes of your heart may be enlightened" (Eph. 1:18). The eyes of "your" heart? Yes, our heart can see. Our eyes and heart don't work independently but function together to form our perspective.

Jesus said "everyone who looks at a woman with lust for her has already committed adultery with her in his heart" (Matt. 5:28). It's not seeing the woman that makes it adulterous. It's the *way* the man looks at her, which is determined by the spiritual condition of his heart. As he views her through *lust glasses*, he commits adultery in his heart. His sinful attitude contaminates the lens through which he views a woman. If he looked at her with a pure heart, he wouldn't be committing adultery.

This also applies to the way we view everything in life. Our perspective is not what we see, but *the way* we see it. Sin pollutes our vision, causing us to misinterpret what we observe. Ungodly attitudes can seize control of our heart, perverting our perspective.

Adulterers behold other people with "eyes full of adultery" (2 Pet. 2:14). Covetous people view others' possessions through "envious" eyes (Matt. 20:15). Proud people look through "haughty" eyes and see others as inferior (Prov. 6:17). The "lust of the eyes" makes

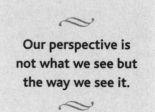

Our perspective is not what we see but the way we see it.

people crave everything they see (1 John 2:16). Their eyes are merely extensions of their hearts.

The condition of our hearts governs the way we view our world. We don't see things as *they* are but as *we* are. As the attitude in our heart changes, how we look at things also changes. The only way to correct our perspectives is by having a transformation of heart. Jesus said, "Blessed are the pure in heart, for they shall see God" (Matt. 5:8). Clarity of vision requires a clean window to look through.

A Change of Heart

Christiaan Barnard of South Africa was the first doctor to successfully perform a heart transplant operation. One day he was talking to his second transplant patient, Philip Blaiberg, and asked him if he would like to see his old heart—the one the doctor had removed. Dr. Barnard took a glass jar containing Blaiberg's old heart off a shelf and handed it to him.

For the first time in history, a man actually looked at his own heart. The patient stared in silence realizing the significance of the moment. Blaiberg then made an interesting comment: "So that is the old heart that caused me so much trouble."[4]

What if God were to show us our hearts? Our spiritual hearts will give us more trouble than our physical hearts. That's why we need a new heart from above.

God the Father wants to transplant His holy heart into us so that we can think His thoughts, feel what He feels, and see through His eyes. Long ago He made a promise: "I will give you a new heart and put a new spirit within you" (Ezek. 36:26). No one can view this life with the proper perspective without a heavenly heart transplant. We can receive a new heart from above by placing our faith and trust in Jesus Christ.

∼ I Once Was Blind, But Now I Squint

When I gave my life to Christ and become a Christian, my eyes had difficulty adjusting to the light after being in darkness. It took time to get used to the light. I once was blind, but now I was squinting. After my eyes adjusted to the light, I was able to see things more clearly than ever before.

Although God gives each new believer a new heart, our perspective still needs to be transformed. He will change us a little at a time, from one degree of glory to another.

> To this day whenever Moses is read, a veil lies over their heart; but whenever a man turns to the Lord, the veil is taken away. . . . But we all, with unveiled face, beholding as in a mirror the glory of the Lord, are being transformed into the same image from glory to glory, just as from the Lord, the Spirit (2 Cor. 3:15, 16, 18).

This principle of transformation is demonstrated by one of the miracles Christ performed. A blind man was once brought to Him to have his eyes opened.

> After spitting on his eyes and laying His hands on him, He asked him, "Do you see anything?" And he looked up and said, "I see men, for *I see them like trees,* walking around." Then again He laid His hands on his eyes; and he looked intently and was restored, and *began to see everything clearly* (Mark 8:23–25, emphasis by author).

Isn't it amazing? The saliva of Jesus can open more blind eyes than all the eye surgeons in the world! In this incident, Christ did the healing in two stages. First, He opened his eyes.

The man could see people, but with blurred vision. Jesus touched him a second time so he could see clearly.

Perhaps Jesus performed this miracle in stages so it could be an object lesson. Healing doesn't always occur instantaneously. Here, the formerly blind man saw people as if they were walking trees. He needed another touch from Jesus to sharpen his focus.

Seeing men as trees can be a problem for us as well . . . especially for lumberjacks. Even after gaining spiritual sight, we still have problems with the way we perceive things. Wicked attitudes in our hearts create the glasses we look through. We must take off our glasses to correctly view our situations.

Although we only need one touch from Christ to open our eyes, we need continual help from heaven to straighten out our twisted perspectives.

In the next section I'll examine your eyes to find out what types of glasses you might be wearing, and then I'll explain how to take them off.

What you discover might be an eye-opener.

PART 2

Distorted Perspectives

E DITH AND SHIRLEY were having coffee one morning. Shirley looked out the window and was awestruck by the sun shining on the flower garden.

"Wow, it's beautiful out there!"

"Yeah," Edith replied, "but look at all the dirt on the window."

Which do you see? The dirt on the window or the flowers in the garden?

Edith sees dirt because she looks through pessimist glasses.

As you read the next twelve chapters, ask yourselves if you're wearing any spectacles that can distort your perspective.

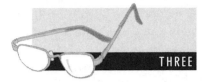

THREE

Discontentment Glasses: In Search of Greener Grass

Next to faith this is the highest art—to be content with the calling in which God has placed you.

~MARTIN LUTHER

I ALWAYS BECOME dissatisfied when I look through my *discontentment glasses*. They filter out God's blessings so I can't see all the good things I have and magnify my problems so they look bigger than they really are. A restless spirit compels me to search elsewhere for a better environment. When I'm discontented, I become so unhappy with my current situation that I'll do almost anything to get out of it.

Have you ever worn these glasses?

Several years ago my friend, Phil, interviewed for a job in Wichita, Kansas. After thoroughly researching the situation, he wasn't sure what to do. He had grown tired of his current job and wanted to move away, but something didn't seem right about this new potential employer—Phil suspected some possible problems. Reluctantly, he withdrew his name from consideration and remained at his job.

For the next two years, Phil continually kicked himself for turning down the job. Every time something went wrong at his workplace, he thought about how happy he would've been if he had taken the position in Wichita.

Then one day, on a flight to Chicago, a businessman sat down next to him. As they conversed, Phil asked him what he did for a living. The man shared he had taken a job two years earlier in Wichita but absolutely hated it—almost daily there was trouble in the office. It didn't take long for Phil to realize that this man had accepted the position at the company where he had applied two years earlier.

> Discontentment always searches for the nearest exit sign.

Phil was flabbergasted. For two long years he thought he had made a mistake by turning down the job. Instead, he discovered that God had protected him from a horrible nightmare. Seemingly, the Lord had arranged this divine appointment to reveal the agony he would've experienced had he taken the job.

The grass looks greener on the other side of the fence, especially when we're looking through discontentment glasses. Discontentment always searches for the nearest exit sign. That's what makes it so dangerous. It pushes us into making foolish decisions that we'll later regret.

∼ Side Effects

Whenever I look through my discontentment glasses, my life becomes miserable. I'm restless and never satisfied. Peace turns into pandemonium. My ability to correctly evaluate is thrown out of whack.

These glasses can impair vision in several ways:

Discontentment creates an imaginary world.

The lenses of discontentment make me see myself as living in horrible conditions. I imagine that everyone else lives in a problem-free world. At least, that's the way it seems. While attending a men's retreat I was able to talk with a successful author. My first book was about to be published, so I had some questions I wanted answered.

"Do you pastor a church and write in your spare time or do you write full-time?" I asked.

"I write full-time."

My first thought was, *This guy has it made. He doesn't have problems like the ones I have to handle.*

"Where do you live?" I asked.

He named a town in Colorado.

Wow. I bet he has a big cabin up in the mountains. Every morning he pours a cup of coffee, goes out on his porch to watch the deer feed in the valley, and writes best-selling books on his laptop computer. That's a great life.

After answering some of my other questions, I thanked him for his time.

For the next year I often thought about how great it would be to trade places with him. Whenever I went through a difficult time, discontentment reared its ugly head. I pictured him sitting on his porch with a panoramic view of the mountains, drinking coffee, and tapping away at his computer. *One of these days*, I thought, *I'm going to have my own cabin surrounded by mountains where I can write books.*

Of course, he never told me he lived in such a place, but that's the perfect world I envisioned. When I'm wearing my discontentment glasses, it's easy to view everyone but me living in paradise.

A year later, the time came for the men's conference. I couldn't attend because of a scheduling conflict. However, several men in our church went to the retreat. When they returned, one of the men told me, "You missed a great weekend."

"I did? What happened?"

"Well, one of the attendees was an author who came last year but has fallen on hard times since then." He told me his name and it was the same author I had talked with the previous year.

"His books haven't been selling, and he hasn't made a mortgage payment in months. The bank is about to foreclose on his house. He was discouraged and didn't know how he was going to get out of the hole.

"The men at the retreat got together, took up an offering, and raised enough money to pay off his debt. God met this fellow's need, and everyone at the retreat received a blessing for helping him. It was incredible."

I was stunned. For the past year I had pictured this author living in a conjured-up cabin on a mythical mountain sipping Starbucks®, free from life's problems. And it wasn't true. I didn't realize that even successful authors aren't exempt from trials.[1]

God is going to make sure that we never live in a place where everything goes our way. That place doesn't exist, except in our mind. Even if it did exist, He wouldn't let us live there. He's calling us to growth, not hibernation.

Do you view everyone else as living in a world that's better than yours? If so, discontentment is distorting your vision.

Discontentment produces an insatiable craving for more.

Someone once asked a multimillionaire how much was enough. He replied, "Just a little bit more."

A discontented person can't remain satisfied for long. Collecting more empty glasses will never quench a person's thirst. Only by filling the inward emptiness will one find true happiness.

A beggar on a street corner commented to his friends, "If I had a hundred dollars, I would never complain again." A businessman walking by overheard his statement and interrupted the conversation.

"Excuse me," the man said. "Did you say if you had a hundred dollars, you would never complain again?"

The beggar replied, "You heard right, mister."

The man pulled out his wallet, handed him a hundred dollars, and said, "I'm glad I can have a small part in bringing happiness to the world."

After the man walked away, the beggar turned to his friends and remarked, "I wish I had asked for two hundred dollars!"

When we're discontented, we're never satisfied with what we receive because our problem is internal. We assume that we could capture contentment if we'd just acquire a little bit more.

Sometimes more is better . . . and sometimes less is better. "Better is a little with the fear of the Lord than great treasure and turmoil with it" (Prov. 15:16). Our attitude takes a higher priority than the amount. Financial poverty with a contented heart is better than having material abundance with a discontented spirit. Why would God want to give us more if we don't appreciate what we already have? Money isn't the issue—the problem is a restless heart.

If someone offered you ten million dollars to be miserable for the rest of your life, would you take it? Only a fool would accept such a proposal. Charles Spurgeon said, "It is not how much we have but how much we enjoy that makes happiness." If we haven't learned to be happy with what we already have, then it doesn't matter how much we accumulate. We won't be able to enjoy it.

True contentment only comes from God's blessing on our life. "It is the blessing of the Lord that makes rich, and He adds no sorrow to it" (Prov. 10:22). A contented person is never poor, and a discontented person is never rich.

Learn to be happy regardless of your circumstances, and then you'll always have a good attitude no matter what happens to you.

Discontentment compels a person to run from God's will.

God instructed Jonah to preach to the people of Nineveh that judgment was coming soon. Although Jonah was God's prophet, he despised his divine assignment. The Ninevites weren't exactly the friendliest neighbors on the block. When they conquered in battle, they cut off their enemies' heads and set the women and children on fire. If they took prisoners, they poked out their eyes and cut out their tongues. Jonah wasn't ready to be blind and dumb at such a young age. Rather than obeying, he fled in the opposite direction.

> **Discontentment points us to a place where God isn't leading.**

Plenty of people today are running right behind Jonah, following in his footsteps. Discontentment will always point one to the path of least resistance. Usually it's a place where God isn't leading.

Jonah hurries down to the travel agency and picks up a brochure. Through his discontentment glasses he reads these appealing points of interest:

FLEEING FROM THE PRESENCE OF THE LORD?
IN SEARCH OF GREENER GRASS?
ESCAPE TO THE VACATION CAPITAL OF
THE WORLD—*TARSHISH.*

- Get away from annoying calls from God.
- Over 3,000 miles from Nineveh.
- Transportation provided by the Backslide Ship.
- Discount prices available for disobedient prophets.

Jonah buys a one-way ticket to Tarshish and is assigned a third-class seat in the lower deck.

Where is your Tarshish? Everybody has a mythical paradise in mind—where the grass is greener, the flowers are prettier, and the sun shines brighter.

Is it another job?

Some other place to live?

A different spouse?

Discontentment stirs up restlessness in our hearts, prodding us to escape from our responsibilities.

But the trip to Tarshish never goes as planned. Jonah wants smooth sailing. God sends stormy seas. Jonah wants understanding fellow travelers, but they toss him overboard instead. God appoints an enormous fish to swallow him. Jonah is assigned a third-class seat in the lower intestine.

Nineveh starts looking like Nirvana when compared to whale's innards. The world's first submarine gives Jonah a one-way trip back to Israel. The fish vomits him onto shore, which is preferable to exiting a whale the other way.

Jonah decides to obey God.
Ninevites repent. God halts judgment.
Jonah still isn't happy. He forgets to remove his discontentment glasses.

Removing these glasses requires a deliberate act of the will. The process begins by enrolling in Contentment University.

~ Take Off Your Glasses

Contentment doesn't come naturally. It's an acquired attitude. Even the apostle Paul had to *learn* the secret of being content. He earned his master's degree at Contentment University. He said,

> I have learned to be content in whatever circumstances I am. I know how to get along with humble means, and I also know how to live in prosperity; in any and every circumstance I have learned the secret of being filled and going hungry, both of having abundance and suffering need (Phil. 4:11, 12).

Contentment University, an institution of higher learning, educates its students in a variety of situations. The school of adversity assigns lessons under the most unfortunate circumstances. The instructors are harsh, the tests stressful.

The school of prosperity, on the other hand, tutors its students in the lap of luxury. Most people are eager to sign up for these classes. They believe the way to achieve contentment is to always have agreeable circumstances. Unfortunately, many people have everything they want but still aren't happy. They've flunked out of the school of prosperity.

That's why we must listen to the instructors in both schools. Paul said, "I know how to be abased, and I know how to abound" (Phil. 4:12, KJV). He learned how to endure trouble in the school of adversity, and enjoy treasure in the school of prosperity.

In the same way, we will graduate with the highest degree of contentment by learning three lessons:

Lesson #1: Seek out God's will, not greener grass.

Discontentment will send you on an endless search for greener grass, but it always takes you to the wrong places. In Psalm 23, David points to the only place where a person will find greener grass. He says, "The Lord is my shepherd, I shall not want. He makes me lie down in green pastures" (Ps. 23:1, 2). You will graze in green pastures only by following the Shepherd's leading. The grass is always greenest in the center of God's will.

The Lord doesn't make us run all over the world trying to find the greener grass. He promises to lead us to green pasture and then invites us to lie down in it. Discontentment refuses to rest in God's will and insists that we look elsewhere for greener grass.

> The grass is always greenest in the center of God's will.

In the 1800s a prospector went to California in search of his fortune. He spent his entire life scouring the mountains for gold, only to die as a pauper. When they were digging the grave behind his house to bury him . . . do I really need to finish the story?

Sometimes the gold we're searching for is in our own backyard. We don't need to search the world over to find happiness. We simply need to follow wherever the Shepherd leads and then lie down and rest in God's will. If the Shepherd isn't leading us to another grazing ground, then we must make the best of our present pasture.

Lesson #2: Be happy with your situation—no matter what it is.

Contentment is not having everything you want—it's wanting everything you have. A more luxurious golf course won't make you a better golfer. A better environment won't remove your discontentment glasses. True contentment can be found only inside your heart, not in your outward surroundings.

A husband and wife enjoyed playing "Here's How I'd Remodel That House" game as they traveled. They would take turns picking out certain houses and explain how they would remodel them. One day as they were out driving, they saw an old, dilapidated house that looked like it had been abandoned. The husband stopped in front of the house and said, "I tell you what I'd do with that shack. I'd bulldoze it down and start over."

At that moment, an elderly man stepped out of the house onto the front porch. With a big smile on his face, the old man waved at them as though they were long-lost friends. The couple waved back and then drove on down the road.

The husband said, "Do you think he would have been that friendly if he knew what I said about his house?"

After a long pause the wife replied, "Probably so!"

The happiest people in the world are those who don't allow anything or anyone to steal their joy. It doesn't matter whether we live in a shack in the school of adversity or a mansion in the school of prosperity, happiness is possible in any situation—if we will get the right perspec-

> Contentment is not having everything you want—it's wanting everything you have.

tive. Contentment in life is not found in a perfect set of circumstances but by *choosing to be happy in every situation.*

Lesson #3: Play the cards that have been dealt to you.

Accept the fact that life isn't always fair. The sooner you learn that lesson, the better. If you look for life to be fair, you'll always be angry. That's why Paul said in effect, "I've learned to accept the fact that life isn't fair, and that's OK. I'm serving God, not my circumstances. I've learned to play the cards that have been dealt to me."

When playing cards, everyone is dealt a different hand. Everybody in life is playing a different set of cards. Some people are holding good cards, while others have been dealt bad hands.

Maybe you were laid off your job unexpectedly. Perhaps you're suffering from a divorce or were hurt in an accident. You might be upset because other card players have good hands, or maybe they've been cheating—and are doing exceptionally well as a result. Although you've been dealt a bad hand, you must still play your cards. The game of life goes on despite crooked dealers and stacked decks.

Although we might not be responsible for the cards we hold, we are responsible for the way we play them. The secret of contentment is to cheerfully play the cards that we've been dealt. We must stop complaining about our bad hand and continue to play the game, trusting the Lord in spite of circumstances. God promises that each believer will have a winning hand in the end. "We know that God causes all things to work together for good to those who love God, to those who are called according to His purpose" (Rom. 8:28).

When we take off our discontentment glasses, we come to a startling realization—the grass is greener on our side of the fence!

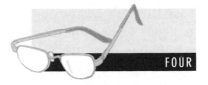

Pessimist Glasses:
Treasure Hunting

The way we choose to see the world creates the world we see.

~ BARRY NEAL KAUFMAN

ROY PARRINO has a job that most people probably wouldn't have on their career wish list. Roy works in a sewer in Orange County, California. He spends his days cleaning out miles of sewer lines in the Los Angeles area—braving toxic fumes, avoiding discarded syringes, and wading through filthy muck that's been flushed down toilets.

"You really have to psych your mind up for it," Parrino says. "Remember, you're going into the filthiest environment there is. It's like being in a big toilet."

Maybe you feel like you're in a sewer right now. You're stuck in an unwanted job, surrounded by intolerable people. You're braving toxic attitudes, avoiding discarded relationships, and trying to fix unsolicited problems. It's tempting to look through *pessimist glasses* when you're surrounded by repugnant environments and repulsive people.

If your heart isn't in tune with God, you'll look for the worst in your situation. You'll overlook the good things you have and gripe about not having enough. When negativity consumes your heart, your perspective gradually deteriorates, plunging you into the sewer of pessimism.

Meet the princess of pessimism, Ima Whiner. She gripes. She complains. She looks for the negative in every situation. Even the Twenty-third Psalm isn't protected from her scrutiny.

A Pessimist's Commentary on Psalm 23
By Ima Whiner

The Lord is my shepherd, I shall not want.

"Shall not want"? Give me a break. I want lots of things. I'd like to have a nicer house, a better job, and a pay raise. I want people to do what I say when I say. And I wouldn't mind winning the lottery either.

He makes me lie down in green pastures; He leads me beside quiet waters.

I have a problem with the words "makes me." That sounds a bit legalistic to me. First you say I can't want things; now you're making me do things.

He restores my soul; He guides me in the paths of righteousness for His name's sake.

I don't want to be guided down the paths of righteousness. I prefer the more scenic routes. How about leading me to Hawaii for a change? What about Vegas? I'm getting a little tired of the paths of righteousness. The next thing you know, you'll be leading me through a dark valley.

Even though I walk through the valley of the shadow of death, I fear no evil, for You are with me.

What am I doing walking through the valley of the shadow of death? I thought I was supposed to be lying down in green pastures. Did you take a wrong turn, or what? And you call yourself a Shepherd?

Your rod and Your staff, they comfort me.

To tell you the truth, a rod and staff are not my idea of comfort. A rod and reel I'll take. A back massage would be even better. Skip the rod and staff.

You prepare a table before me in the presence of my enemies.

Great. Out of all the restaurants in the world, you choose the one where my enemies like to eat. I'm sure I'll relish every bite of that meal!

You have anointed my head with oil; My cup overflows.

I don't want any oil on my head. I prefer shampoo. And for goodness sake, can't you stop pouring before my cup overflows? What kind of waiter are you anyway? How would you like to have hot coffee spilled all over your hand?

Surely goodness and loving-kindness will follow me all the days of my life, and I will dwell in the house of the Lord forever.

I don't want to be confined to a house forever. That sounds like a prison. It might be nice to step outside once every thousand years or so. I never will understand why so many people love the Twenty-third Psalm.

Do you view your circumstances like Ima Whiner?

⁓ Zooming In

Although we may not choose our circumstances, we do choose how we view them. To improve our outlook, we must go treasure hunting. Every situation has both good and bad, but we decide which we look at.

Our heart works like a video camera. The cameraman inside our heart points the camera to what we want to focus on. He can zoom in on an object to help us examine it up close, or zoom out to give us a bigger perspective. As we travel through life, the cameraman inside our heart is constantly zooming in on positive or negative objects.

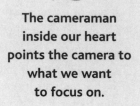

The cameraman inside our heart points the camera to what we want to focus on.

Long ago a king called two servants before his throne. He told the first, "I want you to travel throughout my kingdom and bring back a sample of every weed you can find." He told the second, "I want you to journey throughout my kingdom and bring back a sample of every flower you can find."

Six months later, the first servant returned. The king asked, "Have you carried out my command?" The servant answered, "I have, and I'm amazed to find so many weeds. In fact, there's nothing but weeds in your kingdom."

A few minutes later, the second servant returned. The king asked him, "Have you carried out my command?" He answered, "I have, and I'm amazed to find so many beautiful flowers. In fact, there's nothing but flowers in your kingdom."[1]

Jesus said, "Seek, and you will find" (Luke 11:9). Whatever we seek, we'll find. Zoom in on weeds, and we won't see flowers. Zoom in on flowers, and we won't see weeds.

Moses sent twelve spies into the land of Canaan to bring back a report. Ten zoomed in on weeds. Two saw flowers. Although all twelve men scoped out the same property, they focused on different things and gave opposite reports. Ten looked at the land flowing with milk and honey and saw calories and cholesterol. Joshua and Caleb inspected the same piece of real estate and saw a future homeland.

Every day God asks us to report on the land where we live. In each situation, we must decide whether we're going to zoom in on weeds or flowers. Like those spies from thousands of years ago, about ten out of twelve people today choose to make their lives miserable by looking for what's wrong.

Are you looking through pessimistic glasses? Avoid a negative attitude at all costs. Pessimism breeds other self-destructive attitudes, such as fear, complaining, discouragement, depression, doubt, cynicism, and criticism.

～ You Might Be a Pessimist . . .

If you expect the worst to happen

A man decided to start a hot dog business. He bought a cart, filled it with hot dogs, and pushed it down a busy city street during the lunch hour. He sold out, so he ordered more from his supplier. As the weeks passed, he kept expanding his business and became a successful vendor.

One day his son came home from college and gave him some advice.

"Dad, don't you know what's going on in the business world? Things are bad. We're in a depression."

His father replied, "We are? I guess I'd better cut back on my supply of hot dogs."

So he did. He reduced his inventory, ordering only minimum quantities. Because he kept running out, his frustrated customers stopped buying from him. Several months later he shut down his business.

That night he called his son at college and said, "Son, you were right. We are in a depression!"

The way you choose to see the world creates the world you see. Pessimists expect the worst to happen, which often becomes a self-fulfilling prophecy. Negative attitudes can produce negative circumstances. Looking through pessimist glasses will create a depressing world to live in, just like the hot dog business.

If you have a narrow perspective

Pessimist glasses restrict your perspective, giving you tunnel vision, and causing you to miss the big picture.

A motivational expert lectured a group of business professionals about depression. She took a large sheet of white paper, drew a small black dot in the middle, and posted it on a bulletin board in front of the class. She asked a man on the front row what he saw.

"A black spot," he responded.

A woman seated in the back raised her hand and said, "I would say it's more accurately called a little dot."

The lecturer asked if anyone else could describe what he or she saw. A man blurted out, "A speck."

She told the class, "You all saw the little black dot, but none of you noticed the big white sheet of paper. That's my speech. You can all go home now."

You will become depressed if you get so absorbed with minute details that you miss the big picture. A closed-in viewpoint narrows your perspective, leaving God outside your scope of vision. To get the proper perspective, the cameraman in your heart must zoom out, which brings God's blessings into view.

If you focus on failing instead of succeeding

Optimists light candles. Pessimists blow them out.

Optimism lifts up. Pessimism pulls down.

Optimists see success. Pessimists focus on failure.

Karl Wallenda of the Flying Wallendas was famous for his tightrope walking. Throughout his career, he continually amazed the crowds with his uncanny balance. His career came to an end in 1978 in San Juan, Puerto Rico, when he plunged to his death while crossing a seventy-five-foot-high cable between two hotels. When his wife was later asked why he fell, she gave an interesting explanation. "All Karl thought about for three straight months prior to his accident was falling. It was the first time he's ever thought about that, and it seemed to me that he put all his energies into not falling rather than walking the tightrope."

Wallenda slipped because his focus was on falling. For the last three months of his life, he viewed tightrope walking through pessimist glasses. While many people affirm the power of positive thinking, very few realize the destructive power of negative thinking. Focusing on failure can bring about serious downfalls in business, marriage, and relationships.

Don't let the fear of falling control your thinking. As you walk over the tightrope of life, keep your eyes fixed on Jesus. He will lead you with assurance to the other side.

If you frequently complain

The only happy pessimist is an unhappy pessimist. People who gripe about everything are looking through pessimist glasses.

A new arrival in heaven was surprised to see a suggestion box along Main Street. He asked an angel standing nearby, "If everyone's happy in heaven, why is there a suggestion box here?"

The angel replied, "Because some people aren't happy unless they're complaining."

A pessimistic perspective on life always produces grumbling. I can't find any verse in the Bible saying the Lord will bless whining. Complaining is a prayer wherein you ask God to take away your blessings.

> Complaining is a prayer wherein you ask the Lord to take away your blessings.

ᔈ Take Off Your Glasses

Jesus told His disciples, "Blessed are your eyes, because they see" (Matt. 13:16). Do you want your eyes blessed? Look for the best in your situation. Here are three ways:

1. Take control of your thoughts.

You can't defeat pessimism without first seizing control of your thought life.

The story is told of a little girl who whined, one day, from the time she woke up until she went to sleep that night. In stark contrast, the next day she was in a cheerful mood. Her mother asked, "Why are you so happy today? Yesterday you had a horrible attitude."

"Yesterday my thoughts pushed me around. Today I decided to push them around."

The apostle Paul, the ultimate Biblical optimist, knew how to push around his thoughts:

> Whatever is true, whatever is honorable, whatever is right, whatever is pure, whatever is lovely, whatever is of good repute, if there is any excellence and if anything worthy of praise *let your mind dwell on these things* (Phil. 4:8, author's emphasis.)

When a sponge is full of water, it can't absorb any more because it's saturated. When your mind is saturated with godly thoughts, you won't absorb pessimistic ideas. As long as you keep thinking about what's good, you'll have peace of mind. But if you start pondering how life is unfair, you exchange joy for anguish.

One day my wife, Cindy, refueled our car at a small Texas filling station. Instead of driving up to the self-service pump, she accidentally pulled up to a full-service pump. She didn't realize the luxury service cost an extra fifty cents per gallon until she paid for the gas. What a shocking surprise!

That extra fifty cents per gallon surely has to be a violation of some federal law, I thought. I slipped on my pessimist glasses and quickly calculated that the extra seven dollars she spent on full service would have taken our vehicle 128.33 miles farther down the road if she had bought self-service gas. The "full-service gas station robbery" had me fuming for several hours.

As I was mulling over this terrible injustice, God showed me what I had done. I had sold my joy for seven dollars! I never realized how cheaply I would surrender something so valuable. Just as Esau exchanged his birthright for a bowl of soup, I exchanged my joy for seven dollars' worth of gas.

God used that incident to teach me how focusing on little grievances can steal a lot of joy. I decided right then that I wouldn't forfeit my happiness so easily again. My joy is too precious to allow the thief of pessimism to pickpocket it.

What's stealing your joy? At what price are you willing to relinquish your happiness? It may be someone pulling in front of you on the highway or a small incident at work. It could be a misplaced remote control, a flat tire, or someone's unkind word spoken to you. Focusing on the negative side of any situation will cause you to forfeit your joy.

> I had sold my joy for seven dollars.

2. Give thanks for all things.

The quickest way to kill pessimism is with the weapon of thankfulness. Paul instructed, "In everything give thanks; for this is God's will for you in Christ Jesus" (1 Thess. 5:18).

Thanking the Lord when things aren't going well is a statement of faith, declaring that we believe God is in control. Every time we thank the Lord, we acknowledge our trust in Him despite what we see.

Thankfulness has incredible power—the ability to turn our attitude around. Joy is a by-product of gratefulness, and pessimism can't reside inside a joyful heart. In chapter 16 I will explain how to be thankful for all things.

3. Zoom in on blessings.

Being optimistic doesn't mean to ignore reality but to purposely zoom in on the best in every situation. God wants us to look for buried treasure, even in bad situations.

> Thanking the Lord when things aren't going well is a statement of faith.

I know what you're thinking. How can Roy Parrino find treasure in his occupation? How is it possible to be an optimist while working in a sewer?

The first day Roy descended into his "big toilet" he emerged holding a two-carat topaz ring. Parrino has found necklaces, bracelets, and diamond rings while working in sewers. Although he's saturated in sewage, Roy doesn't focus on filth because he's too busy hunting for diamonds.

You, too, can discover treasure in life's septic tank. No matter how horrible your circumstances may appear— a hidden jewel lies buried and calls out for you to find it. When surrounded by sewage, remember one important nugget of truth: You can find diamonds in a sewer if you'll look for them.

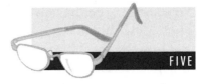

FIVE

Rejection Glasses:
The Angel Inside the Marble

My father carries around the picture of the kid that came with his wallet.

~RODNEY DANGERFIELD

ITALIAN SCULPTOR Michelangelo stared at a block of marble that had been rejected by another artist. A friend approached him and asked what he was looking at.

Michelangelo replied, "An angel."

He was able to see what others couldn't and chiseled an angel out of the stone that another sculptor rejected.

Two thousand years ago a different stone, Jesus Christ, felt the sting of rejection, but retained His perfect perspective on life. Jesus knew His Father was in complete control of every bad thing that happened to Him and had a plan to chisel something good out of it. Matthew tells us "The stone which the builders rejected, this became the chief cornerstone. This came about from the Lord, and it is *marvelous in our eyes*" (Matt. 21:42, author's emphasis).

From the Lord? Marvelous?

Not the rejection. The other part of the verse: "This became the chief cornerstone." Although people rejected Jesus, His Father sculpted Him as the foundation for the Church.

What enemies may plan for evil, God intends for good (see Gen. 50:20). The Heavenly Father fashioned the rejected Messiah into the world's Savior.

Sure, that's true for Christ. But what about when *we* are rejected? Can God chisel an angel out of the marble for us? If we could actually see God's hand at work, that would truly be "marvelous in our eyes" as well.

∼ Rejecting Rejection

Rejection isn't what happens to us but *how we interpret* what happens to us. It's how we view ourselves in relation to others. Are we so insecure that we can't handle being spurned? Some people are devastated when they aren't accepted.

> ∼
> **Rejection isn't what happens to us but how we interpret what happens to us.**
> ∼

A young salesman became discouraged because he had been rejected by so many customers he approached. He asked a more experienced salesman for some advice.

"Why is it that every time I make a call on someone I get rejected?"

"I just don't understand that," answered the older salesman. "I've been hit on the head, called dirty names, and thrown out the door, but I've never been rejected."

Life would be so much easier if we had a Teflon® perspective like that. Although people hated Jesus, He never put on *rejection glasses*. He chose not to be offended and always looked to His Father to control the outcome.

What we perceive in our hearts determines how we respond. If we're easily offended, we become hypersensitive to rejection. Looking through rejection glasses makes us believe others are avoiding us even when they aren't.

Single people sometimes develop an attitude that no one on planet Earth could possibly love them enough to marry them. This false belief—the "no one will love me" syndrome—leaves God completely out of the picture. It can even build unnecessary barriers, which actually generate more rejection. Because fellowship is built on acceptance, rejection is the primary enemy in establishing healthy relationships.

∾ Grounds for Rejection

How does one acquire a perception of rejection? Rejection germinates in three fertile grounds.

Rejection through "difficult people"

Just because someone rejects us doesn't mean the problem is with us. The problem may be with a dysfunctional person who makes everyone feel incompetent.

When Jimmy came home from school his mother asked, "How do you like your new teacher?"

"She's mean, but she's fair," Jimmy replied.

"What do you mean by that?"

"Well, she's mean, but she's mean to everyone."

Some people are mean to everyone. I call them *difficult people* because they make life hard on others. Since the world contains a high percentage of these impolite individuals, our chances of encountering one are pretty good. Don't take their snubbing as a personal insult. These dysfunctional people are mean to everyone, not just us. They don't know how to kindly respond to others.

We have a choice. We can accept rejection, or we can reject it. If we invite rejection into our hearts, we will feel unwanted, unloved, and unworthy. If we refuse to allow dysfunctional people to bother us, we'll go about our business with peace in our hearts.

When Elizabeth Barrett became the wife of poet Robert Browning, her parents disowned her because they disapproved of the marriage. She continued to write her mother and father regularly for years, telling them how much she loved them.

Elizabeth never received a response from her parents until ten years later, when she received a huge package in the mail. She eagerly opened the box, only to discover it contained every letter she had sent them for a decade—all unopened! Although she desired to be reunited with her parents, they refused to accept her in spite of her many attempts.[1]

Difficult people receive satisfaction by rejecting others. In a morbid sort of way, they try to punish others through their snubbing. Are we destined to a life of unworthiness because we can't gain their approval? I think not. We're called to freedom, not bondage (see Gal. 5:13).

No matter what happens, don't allow dysfunctional people to make you feel unacceptable. Find your acceptance through your relationship with Christ, not through trying to appease someone who cannot be pleased.

Rejection through ourselves

Some people never realize that they themselves are the source of their own rejection. The pastor of a large congregation in Dallas told me about his friend who had visited the church.

His friend told the pastor that he wanted to measure the church's friendliness. "I'll stand in the foyer of your church, and I'm almost certain that no one will shake my hand."

The pastor replied, "We have a friendly church. I know that our members will greet you."

After the church service, his friend stood in the foyer as hundreds of people walked past him. After everyone had left, the pastor asked, "Well, did anyone shake your hand?"

"Not a single person."

The pastor was dumbfounded. "What did you do? You must have done something to keep them from meeting you."

His friend explained that he performed an experiment. "Every time someone started to approach me, I simply looked away and gave the impression I didn't want to meet them. They could sense I was rejecting them, so they turned and walked away."

This man demonstrated why some people never form close friendships. They initiate their own rejection by rolling out an *unwelcome* mat toward others—using gestures like frowning, looking away, crossing arms, or staring at the floor. If this man had warmly smiled at those approaching him, he would have met a number of people.

A cold disposition will sabotage a relationship before it ever gets started. Why would someone want to be our friend if we keep pushing them away with our attitude? Many people don't have a clue that they're causing their own rejection, so they get angry when others don't befriend them. They should actually blame themselves for creating barriers that keep others away.

Rejection through imaginations

Highly sensitive people often struggle with imaginations of rejection. Their overly active imaginations create the rejection they love to hate. Rejected people take "no" for an answer before the question has even been asked. They program their minds to assume that others' responses will always be negative. They look for rejection everywhere—and find it. False imaginations cause them to misinterpret innocent intentions and draw wrong conclusions.

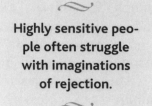

Highly sensitive people often struggle with imaginations of rejection.

One man described a situation in which he imagined that others avoided him. He said, "When I walked into the room, everyone scattered."

The facts came out later. Several people had left the room, but not because he entered it. They had other appointments and needed to leave at that time. Because this man often felt rejected, it was quite easy for him to misunderstand their actions. His rejection glasses made him read between the lines and fill in the blanks. He assumed their exits were due to his entrance into the room, but that simply wasn't the case.

Be careful not to interpret others' actions as rejection. Our assumptions may incorrectly judge their intentions. We might believe certain individuals are trying to avoid us when in reality they aren't. We only *think* they are, like this man who believed people left the room to avoid him.

Imaginations can destroy relationships because they make us assume things that aren't true. I once knew a woman with a history of rejection who was always suspicious of others' motives. A friend once complimented her by saying, "You look nice today."

The woman replied, "Are you saying that I don't look nice every day? You said I look nice *today*. That must mean you think I don't look good on other days."

Her puzzled friend said, "No, I didn't mean that. I just think your dress looks nice. I didn't mean . . ."

"Well, I don't know how to take it any other way. You think I look bad most of the time, don't you?"

Because of her twisted perspective, this woman turned a compliment into an insult. Do you see how viewing others through rejection glasses can sabotage relationships?

It's hard to convince people with imaginations of rejection that they are truly loved. I heard about a wife who felt undeserving of her husband's love. She had a difficult time believing that anyone, including her husband, could ever love her. To test his love, she withdrew and tried to get her husband to reaffirm his acceptance of her. After several episodes of this withdrawal-acceptance cycle, her husband exploded in anger because of her continual need for reassurances. In the wife's mind, his reaction confirmed her imaginations—that he was just pretending to love her. She would never be able to receive her husband's acceptance as long as she looked through rejection glasses.

No amount of affirmation will ever be enough to satisfy the ever-growing demands of someone who views every action as rejection. Only through knowing the truth can a person be set free from these treacherous thoughts (John 8:32).

~ Take Off Your Glasses

You don't need to keep changing jobs, running from relationships, and avoiding certain places. You don't need to forfeit your joy any longer. You can take off your glasses and correct your perception by remembering to do three things.

1. Find peace in God's acceptance, not in others' acceptance.

Paul wrote: "Accept the one who is weak in faith . . . for God has accepted him" (Rom. 14:1, 3). Isn't it encouraging knowing that God accepts us even if no one else does? You must accept the fact that God accepts you. Finding your acceptance in God will help you overcome the painful rejections of dysfunctional people.

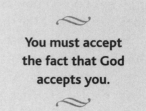

You must accept the fact that God accepts you.

Karen's alcoholic and abusive father abandoned his family when she was two years old. Every Father's Day her mother made her write a card to the father she never knew. Her father never responded. Although Karen's father never accepted her, she finally found a different way to fill the void. She learned at church that God could be her father.

Whenever she went out to play on her roller skates, she yelled, "Hey, God! Look at me!" She felt a special awareness of His presence, as if God were smiling from heaven. Rather than focusing her attention on the man who abandoned her, she directed her affection toward God, who is a father to the fatherless (Ps. 68:5). Although she never received approval from her earthly father, Karen found security through her Heavenly Father. Today she's a spiritually healthy woman, grounded in the love of God.

Turn your spiritual eyes upward to God instead of focusing on others. As long as you're craving acceptance from people, you'll continue to experience the disappointments of rejection. However, if you find your approval in Christ, you can rest in His acceptance of you.

2. View some rejections as closed doors from God.

Jesus instructed His disciples to shake the dust off their feet when the unwelcome mat was rolled out. He said, "Whoever does not receive you, nor heed your words, as you go out of that house or that city, shake off the dust of your feet" (Matt. 10:14). Christ wanted them to move on and leave rejection behind.

That's good advice. Shake off your rejection and look for new opportunities. Don't let even one speck of rejection stick to the soles of your feet, or you'll carry it with you to the next village. Don't allow past rejections to distort your view of future opportunities.

Don't let rejection stick to the soles of your feet, or you'll carry it with you to the next village.

Even though people rejected Jesus, He became the head of the Church. God's plan is not undermined just because we're not warmly welcomed by a few people. Some of your rejections should be viewed as God's way to divert you to something better.

Fifteen different publishing companies rejected my first book proposal. I received letters similar to this one:

Dear Mr. Crockett:

Thank you for submitting your manuscript for our consideration. However, it does not meet our needs at this time.

Christian publishing companies receive approximately 150,000 manuscripts each year.[2] Although many of them are well written, publishing companies can print only a small percentage of what they receive. Editors mail thousands of letters to writers, informing them that their companies are unable to publish their manuscripts. I decided to write a manuscript that my children could keep, even if publishers didn't want it.

Rejection letters from publishers can be quite discouraging. Whenever I received one, I prayed by faith, *Lord, thank you for this rejection letter. This must not be the right company. I ask you to open the right door if you want this published.*

After fifteen rejections, I was running out of publishing companies. One day I received a letter from an editor who loved my manuscript and eventually published my book,[3] which made the Christian Bookseller Association bestseller list, has been translated into Korean and distributed overseas, and is still in print over six years later. God closed doors through those rejection letters to divert me to His door of opportunity.

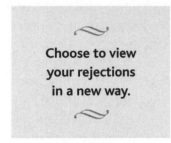

Choose to view your rejections in a new way.

Choose to view your rejections in a new way. An angel is locked up in that block of marble. God may be protecting you from a harmful relationship. A broken engagement can be the hand of God halting one relationship so He can guide you to His choice. Failure to be hired for a job may mean God is directing you to a different assignment. Submit your decisions to the lordship of Jesus Christ, and He will make sure the wrong doors close and the right doors open in His timing.

3. Try to be at peace with those who reject you.

Although you may not become friends with those who reject you, God wants you to make an attempt at peace. "If possible, so far as it depends upon you, be at peace with all men" (Rom. 12:18). Many times it's not possible, but at least you need to make an attempt. If the attempt fails, you can still have peace of mind even if the difficult person doesn't accept you.

Sometimes *your attempt* to make peace will shatter the glasses of rejection. God wants you to obey Him, even if your efforts fail to make peace. You may never be reconciled with someone who holds grudges and refuses to work out differences. However, making this attempt can set you free from your rejection and might even soften the hearts of those who dislike you.

George Sullivan's worst childhood memory was his father holding a knife to his mother's throat, threatening to kill her. George started wearing his rejection glasses on the day his dad moved away from his family. He hated his father and swore he would never be like him. As George grew up, every memory of his dad kindled anger within him. Ironically, the more he thought about his father, the more he became like him.

Forty years later, George attended a Promise Keeper's meeting where the topic of discussion was mending father-son relationships. Now that George was a Christian, God tugged at his heart to forgive his father for the terrible things he had done. He wondered how he could ever have a good relationship with a father who had rejected, abused, and abandoned his own family. Perhaps if he made an attempt to be reconciled, God would set him free from his own hatred.

George began his search to find the man who had abandoned him over four decades before. He decided that if he found him, he would love him unconditionally. After several months of investigation, his leads took him to a bar in Portland, Oregon. He walked into the tavern and asked the bartender, "Is there a man named Bill who's a frequent customer here?" The man pointed to an elderly man sitting at a table by himself.

George pulled up a chair next to the seventy-six-year-old man. He stretched out his hand and introduced himself. "Hi, my name is George."

The old man with the wrinkled face shook his hand, saying, "I have a son named George."

George replied, "I know, Dad. I'm him. How are you doing?"

His father, who had not seen him since he was a boy, choked up with emotion. With tears rolling down his face, he replied in a nervous laugh, "What took you so long to find me?" They hugged and spent the next few hours talking about the last forty years of their lives.

Although he can't explain it, George's rejection glasses fell off that day. He not only made peace with his father but also found peace within his own heart by obeying God. He overcame rejection by accepting his father unconditionally, without demanding that he change to meet his expectations. Reflecting on this new relationship with his father, George said, "God taught me how to be a father to my son. Now He's teaching me how to be a son to my father."

Don't let rejection get you down. Find your acceptance in God. Remember that closed doors are God's way of keeping you out of trouble. Make peace with everyone if you can.

And one more thing—look for the angel inside the marble.

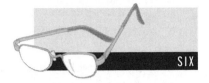

SIX

Envy Glasses:
The Possession Obsession

Envy is the art of counting someone else's blessings instead of your own.

~ RUTH M. WALSH

A RE YOU bothered because your neighbor drives a nicer car than you? Do you crave things that aren't rightfully yours? Do you compare your possessions with others? Do you get upset when you work hard while your fellow employees goof off? If so, you might be looking through *envy glasses*.

I received the following e-mail from a church member who works at a lumberyard:

Dear Pastor Kent,

One of my coworkers is extremely lazy and refuses to do any physical labor. I have always worked my hardest and have been able to keep his laziness from getting to me until today. This afternoon, while I was carrying sheetrock into a house, this lazy guy showed up at the job site. Instead of carrying the sheetrock into the house himself, he made his helper do the work. This made me so mad! Here I was, struggling to do my work, and he was just sitting on his can. I lost my cool, calling him a lazy jerk. I asked if he was going to let the kid do all his work for him. Was I wrong for reacting in this way?

Chris

Here's my reply:

Dear Chris,

Your employer is paying you to do your work, not evaluate his. You aren't just serving your employer but also the Lord (Col. 3:23). I know that it's tempting to get mad at lazy workers, but that's not what you are getting paid for. Take your eyes off your coworker and get them back on what God has called you to do.

Pastor Kent

Chris's conflict with his coworker reminds me of the parable Jesus told about a landowner who hired different groups of people to work in his vineyard. The first group agreed to labor all day for a denarius—the wage for a day's work. The last group of laborers worked for only one hour.

At the end of the day the owner paid all his hired men a denarius. The hired hands who worked only one hour were paid the same wage as those who labored twelve hours. The boss's decision to pay everyone alike outraged the men who had worked all day. Not only did they gripe about their wages, but they thought they deserved considerably more pay because they had worked so many hours. Note the owner's reaction:

> Friend, I am doing you no wrong; did you not agree with me for a denarius? Take what is yours and go, but I wish to give to this last man the same as to you. Is it not lawful for me to do what I wish with what is my own? Or is your *eye envious* because I am generous? (Matt. 20:13–15, author's emphasis).

The first group of workers glared through envy glasses at their fellow employees, comparing wages. Have you ever worn these glasses? Have you ever compared your income with someone else's wages, thinking you deserved more?

∼ Identifying Envy

Sometimes we don't realize we're viewing others through envy lenses. The three C's of envy will help you identify this distorted perspective.

1. Envy compares.

Years ago in Manchester, England, a factory worker was responsible for the whistle that marked the beginning and end of the workday. His job was to make sure the clock was accurate. Every day on his way to work, he stopped by a clock shop and set his watch by an expensive clock displayed in the window. Then he set the factory whistle according to the time on his watch.

The owner of the clock shop noticed him stopping by the window every day and asked him what he was doing. The worker explained that he set the factory clock by the clock in the window so the factory whistle would blow on time.

The owner laughed. "And to think—all this time I've been setting my clock by your factory whistle!"[1]

Do you set your standards by others? Envy compares positions, possessions, and property with those who appear to be more prosperous. Envy compares incomes, like the laborers in the vineyard.

Salary envy: "Charlie gets paid twice as much as I do, and he does half the amount of work."

Mansion envy: "Why can't I have a house like the Millers'?"

Talent envy: "I can sing better than she can, so give me the microphone!"

Envy compares our clothes and our cars, our jobs and our junk. When I look through my envy glasses, I'm bothered if I see others with something better. The psalmist Asaph said, "I envied the arrogant when I saw the prosperity of the wicked" (Ps. 73:3, NIV). Something happens to my heart when I start comparing. I become obsessed with what others possess and ignore the Scripture that tells me to be content with my wages (see Luke 3:14).

Several years ago Dennis Rodman stated he wasn't happy with his $2 million salary from the San Antonio Spurs basketball team: "I've been discredited, treated wrong, and abused for the last several years."

Why wasn't Rodman happy with $2 million? Most people would be thrilled to make that much money. He was envious of the other players who were making $7 million. He slipped on the envy glasses and began comparing his salary with those who made more—not with those who made less.

I've noticed people always envy those who are more fortunate, and never those who are less fortunate. We can get bent out of shape when we start comparing dollars per hour. Viewing others through envy glasses upsets us when their possessions appear to be better than ours.

2. Envy covets.

First, we make comparisons. Next we start coveting what the other person has. Someone once said the world consists of three kinds of people: the "haves," the "have-nots," and the "have-not-paid-for-what-they-haves." I would like to add a fourth group: the "have-to-have-what-the-'haves'-have." Coveting means that I want something that isn't rightfully mine. The apostle Paul struggled with coveting:

> I would not have known about coveting if the Law had not said, "YOU SHALL NOT COVET." But sin, taking opportunity through the commandment, produced in me coveting of every kind (Rom. 7:7, 8).

When I was in sixth grade, I went to a small Lutheran school in New Orleans. Our school didn't have a cafeteria, so each student brought lunch from home and ate it at his or her desk. Every day I carried the same meal in my blue snap-down lunch box:

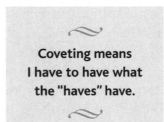

Coveting means
I have to have what
the "haves" have.

Baloney sandwich on white bread. (This was before whole wheat bread was "invented.")

Small bag of potato chips.

Thermos bottle of tomato soup.

Moon pie.

Robbie Buckner sat to my right. He never brought a lunch box to school. At noon each day, his mother delivered him a hamburger from the restaurant down the street. In those days my family was relatively poor, so I got to eat a hamburger at a restaurant only a couple of times a year. Robbie ate them every day.

Each lunch period I was forced to smell his hamburger. I watched in agony as Robbie opened his mouth wide and chewed off a mouthful. I was tortured as I listened to him smack each bite, while I forced a baloney sandwich down my own throat.

> I would not have known about coveting if it weren't for Robbie Buckner's hamburger.

Paul said, "I would not have known about coveting if the Law had not said, 'You shall not covet.'" I would not have known about coveting if it weren't for Robbie Buckner's hamburger.

I memorized the Ten Commandments in this Christian grade school. I could say the tenth by heart:

> You shall not covet your neighbor's house; you shall not covet your neighbor's wife or his male servant or his female servant or his ox or his donkey or anything that belongs to your neighbor (Exod. 20:17).

With my head I learned *not* to covet, but with my heart I learned *how* to covet. I drooled over my neighbor's hamburger every day at lunchtime. I didn't understand how envy could take control of my heart. I started by coveting hamburgers and later, it grew into coveting houses.

I know that hamburgers aren't mentioned in the off-limits list in the tenth commandment. I didn't covet my neighbor's house, wife, servants, ox, or donkey. But that last phrase did me in: "or anything that belongs to your neighbor." Yep, that includes hamburgers.

And who is my neighbor? Anyone outside of me.

Maybe your problem isn't your neighbor's sandwich, but could it be your neighbor's spouse? Adultery begins through coveting. Stealing starts with coveting. Discontentment is born by coveting. And the list goes on. When coveting consumes one's heart, ungodly actions are soon to follow.

> From within, out of the heart of men, proceed the evil thoughts, fornications, thefts, murders, adulteries, *deeds of coveting* and wickedness, as well as deceit, sensuality, *envy*, slander, pride and foolishness (Mark 7:21, 22, author's emphasis).

3. Envy complains.

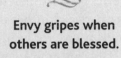

Envy gripes when others are blessed.

The fruit of envy is complaining. Envy always gripes when others are blessed. The first group of workers complained about their wages. The one-hour laborers were paid the same as the all-day workers, which looked like an injustice when viewed through envy glasses.

How did the workers handle this apparent injustice? They complained against the landowner instead of thanking him. They forgot that twelve hours earlier they had agreed to work for one denarius, and the landowner paid them that amount. Their employer wasn't being unfair to the all-day laborers; he was simply being generous to the one-hour workers.

Are you irritated when you work hard while others are goofing off? Many employees today agree to work for a certain wage but then complain when a fellow worker gets paid more. Are you guilty of salary envy? It's easier to complain about what you don't have than be thankful for what you do have. Envy always drains thankfulness from your heart.

~ Take Off Your Glasses

Some people never realize that envy is the source of their strife with others. James 4:1, 2 says, "What is the source of quarrels and conflicts among you? . . . You are *envious* and cannot obtain; so you fight and quarrel." The source of their quarrels wasn't anger but envy.

How do you remove your envy glasses?

1. Love your neighbor, not what your neighbor has.

A wealthy elderly man married a beautiful young woman. Not long afterward, he began to wonder if she married him for his money or love for him. He decided to consult a counselor.

"Doc, my problem is driving me crazy. I need to know if my wife really loves me or if she just married me for my money."

"The answer is simple," the counselor explained. "Give away all your money except just enough to live on. If your wife stays, she loves you. If she leaves, she loves your money."

Envy means you love your neighbor's possessions more than you love your neighbor. Which concerns you the most— your neighbor's material prosperity or their spiritual welfare?

We must stop being obsessed with what others possess. We have no right to covet what another owns. Jesus said, "Beware, and be on your guard against every form of greed; for not even when one has an abundance does his life consist of his possessions" (Luke 12:15).

Quit looking at your neighbor's property, and start caring about their relationship with Christ.

2. See God as your provider.

I have a friend whose brother's salary quadruples my salary. When he told me this, salary envy came knocking at my heart's door. Immediately I felt convicted by the Holy Spirit. Did I really trust God to provide for my daily needs? If so, then I didn't need to covet his salary.

If we see God as our provider, we won't be bothered if someone makes more money than we do. God promises to meet our needs, but not our greeds. Jesus taught us to pray, "Give us this day our daily bread" (Matt. 6:11). He wants us to depend upon Him for provision.

Trust God to supply your daily bread. He never promised to provide yearly bread. He will, however, give you enough to live on today.

God never promised to provide yearly bread.

A rich man promised his son an annual allowance. On a certain day each year, he gave his son one lump sum. After a while, the only time the man saw his son was on the yearly day he received his allowance. He realized his son was taking him for granted.

The father decided to change the plan. Instead of giving him a large sum of money once a year, he distributed a little bit to him on a daily basis. From then on he saw his son every day.[2]

God wants to provide you with daily bread so you will depend on Him every day. Trust Him to provide what you need, and quit worrying about what others have.

3. Be content with your wages.

John the Baptist said, "Be content with your wages" (Luke 3:14). Contentment means being thankful for our salary and living within our means. Being content with our pay doesn't mean we can't have a raise in salary or a promotion at our job.

It does mean we don't get upset when someone else gets a raise or promotion.

Studies by University of Illinois psychologist Ed Diener show that receiving a pay raise temporarily raises people's level of happiness, but then the glow fades. As people get used to having more money, they set loftier goals that often fail to produce long-term happiness. "As you start meeting basic needs, increases in income become less and less important," says Diener.[3]

Researchers found a declining effect of income on happiness at salaries well below $100,000. "Many people say, 'If I only had a million dollars, I'd be happy.' It could be true for an individual, but for most people on average, it appears not to be true."[4]

Money is neither good nor bad, but can be used for either according to our attitude toward it. If we're wealthy, our resources can be utilized to bless others and further God's kingdom. Money should be a tool for serving the Lord, not a source for happiness.

Another study has found that wealth has little effect on happiness. Diana Pidwell, a clinical psychologist, said, "It seems to be the consensus that once you have the basic level of income, then after that it does not make any difference to happiness. There is evidence that there are very wealthy people who are very unhappy. Happiness is a state of mind."[5]

Isn't happiness having the right perspective? Would you like to improve your outlook on life? Take off your glasses and discover the blessings God has already given you. You have it better than you realize.

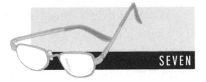

SEVEN

Jealousy Glasses:
Suspicious Eyes

Jealousy sees with opera glasses . . . changing suspicions into truths.

~CERVANTES

DO YOU KNOW the mythical story of Pandora's box? A man gave a woman named Pandora a mysterious box with the instructions not to open it under any circumstances. One day when she was left alone, Pandora's curiosity got the best of her. She lifted the lid to take a peek inside, and count-less heartaches and miseries swarmed about her. Opening the box unleashed the sorrows of the world.

Jealousy is a Pandora's box that opens the door to more evils. James 3:16 says, "Where jealousy and selfish ambition exist, there is disorder and every evil thing." Open the door to jealousy, and other evils will follow—hate, accusations, revenge, strife, and murder, just to name a few.

What's the difference between envy and jealousy? Although they may look alike, they aren't identical twins. Envy wants what belongs to another person. Jealousy clings to its own property, trying not to lose it. Envy is obsessed with possessions, while jealousy is obsessed with a person. Envy craves status; jealousy craves affection. Envy is grounded in covetousness; jealousy is rooted in mistrust.

ENVY	JEALOUSY
Wants what others have	Clings to its own
Is obsessed with possessions	Is obsessed with a person
Craves status	Craves affection
Is grounded in covetousness	Is rooted in mistrust

Jealousy is gripped with the fear that it will lose a loved one. Rooted in suspicion, it views others as threats. Insecure people look through their *jealousy glasses* and accuse their loved ones of misconduct. Jealousy doesn't trust, even when the accused individual is innocent.

Let's suppose Jesus got married while He was on earth. His wife is insanely jealous, even though He is sinless.

His wife says, "I saw you talking to Mary Magdalene yesterday. What were you talking about?"

"It was innocent. I was just telling her about the kingdom of God."

"Oh, is that so? I bet you tell that to all the ladies!"

Joseph's brothers looked through these glasses. "His brothers saw that their father loved him more than all his brothers;

and so they hated him and could not speak to him on friendly terms . . . and his brothers were jealous of him" (Gen. 37:4, 11). Jealousy drove them to plot his murder.

After David killed Goliath, women danced in the streets and sang victory songs. Saul smiled when they sang, "Saul has slain his thousands." He thought, *Hey, they're singing my favorite song!* Then the women sang the second stanza: "And David his ten thousands" (1 Sam. 18:7). Saul's smile turned to scorn. *They think David is ten times better than I am! What will they call me in verse three? Saul the Chicken-Hearted?*

When Saul heard the women exalting David rather than himself, jealousy consumed him. An evil spirit slapped a pair of jealousy glasses on Saul, and he "looked at David with suspicion from that day on" (1 Sam. 18:9). He wore those specs until his dying day.

King Herod looked through jealousy glasses and executed his wife because he suspected she committed adultery. When he heard the King of the Jews was born, he ordered the small children in Bethlehem to be slaughtered. He was jealous of a newborn king.

Can you see the fruit of jealousy? Accusations. Hatred. Murder.

Whether jealousy is caused by unfaithfulness or imaginations, both perceptions will torment the mind and strain relationships.

Years ago as I was dating the young lady who would eventually become my wife, jealous imaginations started flashing through my mind. We were in a long-distance relationship, so the devil tried planting a few doubts and suspicions.

One day as I was being tortured by these thoughts, I picked up God's Word to find help. I opened my Bible to James 3. The following verses jumped out at me:

> If you have bitter jealousy and selfish ambition in your heart, do not be arrogant and so lie against the truth. This wisdom

is not that which comes down from above, but is earthly, natural, *demonic* (James 3:14, 15, author's emphasis).

God's Word had nailed the source of my imaginations. Those tormenting thoughts of jealousy weren't true but were coming straight from the pit of hell. As soon as I realized what was happening—poof!—the demon left. My eyes were opened to the truth, and the truth set me free (see John 8:32).

It's no wonder why the devil deposited those lying thoughts in my mind. He wanted to wreck the relationship between Cindy and me.

And he wants to plant some lies in your mind, too.

∼ Dissecting Jealousy

People become jealous either due to actual unfaithfulness, or perceived disloyalty. God wants to build holy relationships, without infidelity or jealousy. Looking through jealousy glasses can make bad situations even worse. Let's analyze this destructive attitude.

Suspicious

Jealousy is exceedingly mistrustful and will go to ridiculous lengths to confirm suspicions. Chuck Swindoll shares that when he was counseling a young married couple, the husband looked at his wife through jealousy glasses and accused her of cheating on him, even though it wasn't true.

The wife said, "This man is so jealous of me—before he leaves for work in the morning he checks the odometer on my car. Then when he comes home, sometimes even before he comes into the house, he checks it again. If I have driven a few extra miles, he quizzes me during supper."[1]

Checking odometers won't fix marriage problems, but it can compound them. This couple had a serious trust issue that should have been addressed during premarital counseling. Suspicions can be rooted in imaginations or reality. Whatever the source, the problem must be addressed, or it will destroy the relationship.

Threatened

Jealousy usually involves a rival lover. A third party enters the picture, creating a threat to the relationship. The object of affection is usually a person, but not always. It could be a hobby, sport, car, or even a job that becomes the rival lover in the relationship.

John Oresky was a musician who played with some great bands and orchestras. He spent so much time practicing the flute that his wife became jealous, which added to their marital problems. He was giving more attention to his flute than to his wife.

One day John's wife decided to leave him. Oddly, she didn't remove any of the dresses from her closet when she departed. She only took one object with her—his flute. Oresky explained why his wife ran off with his instrument. "It's because she is jealous of that flute."[2]

Jealousy arises from insecurity, viewing others as potential threats. This doesn't mean we should blindly trust everyone, regardless of his or her character. Be discerning. God wants us to protect our spouse because we've been joined together by the marriage covenant. However, we do need to distinguish between what is and what isn't a legitimate threat to the relationship.

Accusative

Jealousy accuses the loved one of misconduct by saying, "Guilty until proven innocent." The accused person must defend his or her innocence. This can be devastating if the accused hasn't done anything wrong. Even if the person is guilty, reacting in a jealous rage only makes the situation worse.

> **The fact is: we cannot make anyone love us.**

The fact is: we can't make anyone love us. We can, however, drive a loved one away by constantly making accusations. Rather than drawing the person closer, a mistrustful attitude sends the loved one running in the other direction. Ironically, the separation is the opposite of what jealousy intends.

Possessiveness is the wrong solution to the jealousy problem. Learn a lesson from the kitchen cupboard—more flies are caught with honey than vinegar.

Sweetness attracts. Sourness repels.

Think about it. We win by wooing, not screaming.

Take Off Your Glasses

Jealousy is an accusatory, ruthless thought that wants to take over the living room of your mind. Although it has no right to be there, it forces itself through the front door and tries to take possession of your house.

There's only one way to get rid of the occupant—by a deliberate act of the will. You must evict the intruder. It won't leave on its own. You must forcefully grab it, throw it out the door, and forbid it from reentering the premises.

1. Don't jump to conclusions.

Jealous imaginations can deceive us. Assumptions will cause us to jump to wrong conclusions, provoking us to take actions that we'll later regret.

Sam and Jacqueline Pritchard started receiving mysterious phone calls to their home in England in the middle of the night. The person on the other end never made a comment. After a long pause, he would hang up.

They changed their phone number to stop the harassing night calls. The stalker changed his tactic. He started sending them obscene and threatening anonymous letters in the mail. The couple discovered their house had been daubed with paint, and their tires were slashed. The Pritchards became prisoners in their own home and spent a small fortune on a security system. They had no idea what they had done to deserve such cruel treatment.

After four months of unexplained terrorism, they finally met the perpetrator. Mr. Pritchard caught James McGhee, a fifty-three-year-old man, while he was damaging their car. As they looked at each other, Pritchard asked him, "Why are you doing this to us?"

The vandal responded, "Oh, no—I've got the wrong man!"

McGhee thought he was terrorizing a different man, who had been spreading rumors about him. He had looked up Pritchard's name and address in the telephone directory and assumed he was the person responsible for slandering him. He got the wrong Pritchard. His erroneous assumption brought misery to the couple for four months.

Jealousy jumps to wrong conclusions, and others suffer as a result. After the damage is done, it's too late. You can stop the insanity by casting down imaginations and "taking every thought captive to the obedience of Christ" (2 Cor. 10:5).

2. Let Jesus be your greatest love.

Jesus said the greatest commandment is to "love the Lord your God with all your heart, and with all your soul, and with all your mind" (Matt. 22:37). Jealousy is more obsessed with a person than with the Lord, causing your affections for that person to become greater than your passion for Christ. When you love God with all your heart, you submit your desires to His lordship.

> Jealousy is obsessed with a person more than the Lord.

> Love is patient, love is kind and is not jealous . . . does not act unbecomingly; it does not seek its own, is not provoked, does not take into account a wrong suffered (1 Cor. 13:4, 5).

Human love can be extremely jealous, act inappropriately, and be easily provoked. God's love, *agape*, does not fly into a rage or yield to provocation.[3] The only way to receive agape is through a personal relationship with Jesus Christ. When Christ becomes ruler of your heart, His love brings your emotions under control.

What is our greatest love? Whom do we think about the most? When Jesus becomes our primary love, everyone else becomes secondary. He needs to rule our hearts—not jealousy.

3. Place your loved one in God's hands.

A person looking through jealousy glasses tries to control a loved one's affections, which only leads to frustration. How can you regulate someone else's feelings when his or her emotions are beyond your control? You can't. The solution is to place your loved one in God's hands through prayer.

Perhaps you're in a dating relationship and are afraid of losing your boyfriend or girlfriend. Trust the Lord that He will give you what's best. Face the reality that the one you now care about might, or might not, be His choice for you. Let Him decide. "No good thing does He withhold from those who walk uprightly" (Ps. 84:11).

Jealousy constructs a cage around a loved one, which becomes a prison. For a dating relationship to work correctly, that person must be *free* to love you—without your coercion or manipulations. Christ wants you to take your hands off the situation and place your loved one into His hands.

You must release your loved one from manipulations and accusations. Of necessity, you need to open the cage and let them go. If the loved one returns, he or she is yours. If the loved one doesn't return, the relationship was never yours to begin with. Releasing your loved one to the Lord and placing your situation in His hands will set you free from the tormenting bondage of jealousy.

The wisdom from below produces bitter jealousy, but the wisdom from above produces purity, peace, and gentleness (see James 3:14–17).

Let me advise you from my own experience—take the thoughts from heaven.

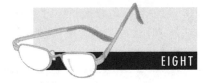

EIGHT

Inferiority Glasses:
I Love Me, I Love Me Not

*I have always wanted to be somebody, but I see now that I
should have been more specific.*

~LILY TOMLIN

I LOVE ME.
I love me not.
I love me.
I love me not.
To love self or not to love self. That is the question. Jesus
said, "You shall love your neighbor as yourself" (Matt. 22:39).
I love me.
He also said, "If anyone comes to Me, and does not hate
his own father and mother and wife and children and broth-
ers and sisters, yes, and even his own life, he cannot be My dis-
ciple" (Luke 14:26).
I love me not.

These two apparently contradicting verses, both spoken by Jesus, makes me wonder, "Should I love me—or love me not? If God loves me, shouldn't I love me?"

And here's a bonus question. If Jesus commanded us to love everyone, why does He now tell us to hate?

No, Jesus wasn't commanding us to despise Mom and Dad. The biblical word "hate" doesn't always mean to "cease loving." In this case, it is used as an idiom of preference, in which one person is preferred over another. When Jesus says that we must hate our relatives and ourselves, He means that we must favor Him above everyone else. Christ wants to lead us rather than letting anyone else control our lives.

However, some people wrongly believe they must hate themselves—the very souls Jesus created and died for. If that were true, we should *want* to go to hell, which would be the ultimate hatred of self. Obviously, that can't be right. We would be fulfilling Satan's will, not God's.

The devil, the master of hate, has been busy in hell's workshop manufacturing *inferiority glasses*. Slip on these glasses, and we'll view ourselves as a worthless creature with no reason to live. Our eyes shift off Christ and onto ourselves. We become focused inwardly instead of upwardly. Inferiority glasses blind us from seeing ourselves as God's unique creation with a wonderful purpose to fulfill.

Author Leanne Payne has said, "If we are busy hating the soul that God loves and is in the process of straightening out, we cannot help others. Our minds will be riveted on ourselves—not on Christ, who is our wholeness."[1]

～ The Comparison Trap

A man told his psychiatrist, "Doc, I think I have an inferiority complex. Please help me."

The doctor ran a series of elaborate tests, then called his patient back into his office to discuss the results.

"Please have a seat," the doctor said. "I've got good news and bad news. The good news is that you don't have an inferiority complex."

"That's great," the relieved man said. "What's the bad news?"

"The bad news is that you really *are* inferior."

Many people try to attain self-worth by comparing themselves with others. They think feeling superior will increase their self-esteem. However, comparison usually makes most people feel inferior. Paul warned about the dangers of using others as a measuring stick when he wrote,

> We are not bold to class or compare ourselves with some of those who commend themselves; but when they measure themselves by themselves and compare themselves with themselves, they are without understanding (2 Cor. 10:12).

Remember the ten spies who brought back a bad report about the Promised Land? They looked through inferiority glasses when they compared themselves with the people in Canaan. They said, "All the people whom we saw in it are men of great size . . . and we became like grasshoppers *in our own sight*, and so we were in their sight" (Num. 13:32, 33, author's emphasis).

The way you see *yourself* determines how you believe others see you. The ten spies saw themselves as grasshoppers ("in our own sight") and believed their enemies also saw them that way ("so we were in their sight"). If you see yourself as inferior, then you believe everyone else sees you as inferior.

> The way you see yourself determines how you believe others see you.

Whenever you measure yourself with others, you wrongly interpret yourself-worth. The comparison trap can be devastating. Someone is always bigger, stronger, faster, and prettier. Just when you think you're winning the rat race, you run into faster rats. It's a frustrating way to live.

∼ Mirror, Mirror, on the Wall

When we look through these glasses into the mirror, we see the most unlovable creature gawking back at us. Inferiority glasses draw our attention to four areas of introspection that produce self-hatred.

> ∼
> **Self-image is the
> self-portrait that
> hangs in the gallery
> of your mind.**
> ∼

1. Physical appearance

Self-image is the way we view ourself. It's the self-portrait that hangs in the gallery of our mind. Some people have considered committing suicide because they hate the way they look. This *is not* the kind of "hating self" that Christ meant.

A popular attraction at carnivals is the crazy house of mirrors. Inside this maze of warped mirrors, we can view our contorted reflections. When we look into these mirrors, our eyes and ears seem to balloon out of proportion. We see ourselves as extremely skinny or overweight. We don't actually look like that, but the warped mirrors make us appear so.

Inferiority's misshapen lenses make us see ourselves like the mirrors in the crazy house. A warped self-image is no closer to reality than the image reflected by the contorted mirrors at the carnival. These glasses make us disgusted with our appearance. We focus on our unsightly features and exaggerate each flaw. My, what big ears, nose, and eyes we have! Dissatisfaction with our appearance can produce hatred toward the God who created us.

A Louis Harris Poll showed that 56 percent of men would like to lose weight, 36 percent want more hair, 34 percent would change their height, 27 percent would hide signs of aging, and 19 percent would like a different nose. Women wanted to make even more changes. Seventy-eight percent of women aren't happy with their weight, 48 percent would hide signs of aging, 37 percent would change their teeth, 34 percent would have different legs, and 18 percent would change their feet.[2]

Do you think having a nearly perfect physical appearance would help our self-esteem? A survey of twelve Hollywood actors and actresses proves it doesn't. They were asked, "If you could change something about your facial features, what would it be?" The answers ranged from four to twelve items per person. These people, admired by millions as the most beautiful and handsome in our society, obviously did not accept themselves. It's not so important what we are but what we think we are.[3]

2. Intelligence

We can't allow our IQ to be the determinant of our self-worth. God makes His Albert Einstein and His Forrest Gump. He has also made sure that no one will ever know everything. Geniuses may excel in one field of expertise but can be quite ignorant in other areas. Will Rogers once said, "Everyone is ignorant, except on different things."

A person's intelligence doesn't necessarily guarantee success in the workplace. Karen Arnold, an assistant professor of education at Boston College, and Terry Denny, a professor emeritus at the University of Illinois, followed eighty-one valedictorians and salutatorians for ten years after their graduations. To the surprise of the researchers, most of these scholars achieved only average success in the workplace. Success can usually be attributed to attitude, diligence, and hard work, not necessarily aptitude.[4]

Intelligence might even hinder us from receiving God's revelation. Depending on our own understanding can deter us from trusting God to lead us (see Prov. 3:5, 6). Jesus prayed, "I praise You, Father, Lord of heaven and earth, that You have hidden these things from the wise and intelligent and have revealed them to infants" (Matt. 11:25). God has made truth so simple that a small child can understand it. God is more concerned with our "I will" than our IQ.

> *God is more concerned with our "I will" than our IQ.*

3. Abilities

The master in the parable of the talents distributed five talents to one slave, two to another, and to another one, "each according to his own ability" (Matt. 25:15). God doesn't give everyone the same abilities. Some people may be extremely gifted in one area, while others are gifted in other ways.

> *God never gave us abilities as a measuring stick to determine our self-worth.*

God never gave us abilities as a measuring stick to determine our self-worth. We've been granted certain capabilities so that we can fulfill our destiny. God has called and equipped us to accomplish His will, not so we can brag about our abilities. God wants us to use our talents and gifts for His glory, not our own glory.

4. Achievement

Self-worth should never be measured by achievement. Several years ago a successful businessman lost over a million dollars in a bad investment. Someone asked him, "How much are you worth now?"

"I'm worth the same as I always was," the businessman replied. "I never calculate my self-worth according to my successes or failures."

While we should work diligently at our jobs, we should never base our worth on performance.

What appears to be an insignificant job in our eyes can actually be of incredible importance to God. Being a servant will make us great (see Mark 10:43). Becoming a slave will elevate us to number one (see Mark 10:44). Even a cup of cold water given in Jesus' name will be rewarded in heaven (see Mark 9:41). Being faithful in little on earth will result in being in charge of much in eternity (see Luke 19:17). Many achievements ignored by this world are highly esteemed by God.

Other reasons for self-hate

People hate themselves for other reasons: Self-pity, feelings of failure, excessive introspection, guilt from past sins, rejection by parents or peers, and lack of purpose in life are just a few. God didn't create us so that we could find reasons to self-destruct. We will never function to our fullest potential as long as we view ourselves as inferior.

⌒ Take Off Your Glasses

Attaining a healthy self-image requires that you see yourself as God sees you. To have a permanent change in perspective, the Holy Spirit must reprogram your heart. Once God changes you within, you can view yourself in a spiritually healthy way.

Inferiority is false humility. How can you get rid of this self-destructive perspective? Several vital steps are necessary to take off your glasses.

1. Die to self.

Paul said, "Realize this, that in the last days difficult times will come. For men will be lovers of self" (2 Tim. 3:1, 2). "Lovers of self" seek to please themselves, feed their egos, and demand their own way. This is usually manifested through self-centeredness, conceit, and the desire to receive attention.

To "hate self" means to hate *selfishness*, not the person God created you to be. Selfishness demands its own way, sees itself as the center of the universe, and opposes the rule of God. Paul said, "I die daily" (1 Cor. 15:31), which meant that he put self-ishness in the grave each day. He also proclaimed, "I have been crucified with Christ; and it is no longer I who live, but Christ lives in me" (Gal. 2:20). Jesus will become real in our lives when we die to selfishness.

Near the end of World War II, newspapers in Japan adver-tised for kamikaze pilots. They searched for volunteers to fly planes on just one mission—to crash into American aircraft carriers. These suicide pilots were strapped in a plane with dynamite and given enough fuel to fly out to sea but not enough to return. Once someone became a kamikaze pilot, he couldn't turn back. Before he departed for his mission, his family gave him a funeral. The pilot attended his own funeral.

Although we're still alive, we need to attend selfishness's funeral every day. Jesus said, "If anyone wishes to come after Me, let him deny himself, and take up his cross daily and follow Me" (Luke 9:23). We don't take up our cross daily to crucify Jesus again but to crucify selfishness. Each morning when we wake up, self wakes up with us and tries to

> It's not what you say about yourself that makes it true but what God says about you.

rule our lives. The cross is where self dies. Crucifying our self-ishness will prevent it from warping our perspective.

2. Accept yourself as God's creation.

Some people have delusions of grandeur, while others have delusions of worthlessness. People who are disgusted with themselves direct their hatred toward God. They angrily shake their fists at Him, complaining, *Why did You make me like this?*

God answers, "The thing molded will not say to the molder, 'Why did you make me like this,' will it?" (Rom. 9:20).

The Lord wants you to accept yourself as His creation. David said, "I will give thanks to You, for I am fearfully and wonderfully made; Wonderful are Your works, and *my soul knows it very well*" (Ps. 139:14, author's emphasis). David not only thanked God for creating him but also realized He did a wonderful job doing so.

You can acquire a healthy self-image by recognizing that God crafted you in your mother's womb and that you're wonderfully made. It's not what you say about yourself that makes it true but what God says about you.

Jesus said you're more valuable than:

- *Birds.* "Consider the ravens, for they neither sow nor reap; they have no storeroom nor barn, and yet God feeds them; how much more valuable you are than the birds!" (Luke 12:24).
- *Many sparrows.* "Do not fear; you are of more value than many sparrows" (Matt. 10:31).
- *Sheep.* "How much more valuable then is a man than a sheep!" (Matt. 12:12).
- *The entire world.* "What will it profit a man if he gains the whole world and forfeits his soul? Or what will a man give in exchange for his soul?" (Matt. 16:26).

Christian psychologist James Michaelson once counseled a woman who felt lonely and abandoned. As she explained how she felt, he couldn't concentrate on what she was saying, because a Scripture kept running through his mind: "It is He who has made us, and not we ourselves" (Ps. 100:3). This verse had no apparent connection with her problem, but he couldn't quit thinking about it.

After she finished talking, she sat in silence waiting for a response. Dr. Michaelson didn't know what to say other than quote the verse, although he realized it might sound foolish since it seemed unrelated to her dilemma.

"I think God wants you to know something," Dr. Michaelson said. " 'It is He who has made us, and not we ourselves.' Does that mean anything to you?"

The woman immediately broke down and cried.

After composing herself, she explained what it meant.

"I didn't tell you this, but my mother got pregnant with me before she was married. All my life I believed that I was a mistake—an unplanned accident—and that God didn't create me. "When you quoted that verse, I pictured in my mind God forming me in my mother's womb. Now I know that God created me and that I'm not a mistake. I'll never be the same again! Thank you, Dr. Michaelson. I'll never forget this day as long as I live!" (as told to the author by Dr. Michaelson).

God knew this woman needed to know she was His marvelous creation and not an accident. Her perspective changed dramatically once she understood that God had crafted her in the womb. Like King David, she discovered God as her Creator.

Can you say, "I am fearfully and wonderfully made"? Does your soul know it very well?

3. Love your neighbor as yourself.

Jesus said, "You shall love your neighbor *as yourself*" (Matt. 22:39). Both you and your neighbors are equally valuable in God's eyes. The way to love your neighbors is to feel their pain when they hurt. You need to take your eyes off yourself, and focus on your neighbors' needs.

My daughter Hannah practiced two long weeks for the high school cheerleader tryouts. She had been a junior varsity cheerleader but wanted to move to the top squad. Only three varsity spots were available in a school of about two thousand students. And Hannah was nervous about competing against the other girls.

"Dad, do you think God wants me to make the varsity squad?" she asked.

"Practice as hard as you can," I answered. "Do your best at the tryouts, and leave the results to God."

Her best friend, Melissa, who was already a varsity cheerleader, practiced with Hannah every day to help her make the varsity team. They had talked about how fun it would be if they could cheer together. Melissa taught her the proper way to jump and encouraged her to always keep a smile on her face. When Hannah became discouraged, Melissa always egged her on with, "You can do it, Hannah! I know you can!"

On the day of the tryouts over a hundred girls showed up to compete for the three spots. That afternoon each girl performed a routine in front of the judges. The results of the competition would be posted at 9:45 p.m. Although each contestant had high hopes of making the squad, all but three would go home heartbroken that evening.

Just before 10:00 p.m., Hannah came bursting in our front door sobbing uncontrollably. Immediately my wife, Cindy, and I jumped out of our chairs and rushed over to comfort her for not making the cheerleading squad. Cindy patted her on the back and said, "It's OK that you didn't make varsity cheerleader. We still love you, and we're proud that you tried."

Hannah continued to cry. She finally settled down and explained what happened.

"Mom and Dad, I *did* make varsity. But Melissa *didn't* make it! The judges demoted her to the junior varsity squad and gave me her place on the varsity. She's devastated. I hurt so badly for her!"

We were stunned. Melissa had gone the extra mile to help Hannah make the varsity team so they could cheer together. We certainly didn't expect this strange turn of events. With hands covering her face, Hannah continued to weep. "I don't want to be a varsity cheerleader now. I want my junior varsity position back so Melissa can stay on varsity. Do you think the judges will let me swap places with her? I love her so much. Now she says she has nothing to live for."

"Hannah, I don't think the judges would allow that," I said.

She realized what she needed to do. Immediately she got up, walked out the front door, and drove to Melissa's house. She wanted to comfort Melissa that night, so she slept on the floor next to her bed. Hannah knew the best thing she could do was to be near her friend during this difficult time.

The next few days Hannah helped her work through her devastation. Melissa put her disappointment behind her and excelled in other ways during her remaining years in high school.

I watched Hannah lead cheers at varsity football and basketball games for the next two years. But that's not what I remember most about her cheerleading career. My fondest memory was the night she slept on the floor of a hurting friend.

When you swap places with others to feel how they hurt, you've taken the first step toward loving your neighbor as yourself.

And you've also learned how to remove your inferiority glasses.

Now, where was I? Oh, yeah . . .

I love me not.

I love me.

NINE

Wounded Glasses:
Sore Spots

A person with a toothache cannot fall in love.

~ SIGMUND FREUD

ONE SUNDAY morning before church I greeted a man as he entered the sanctuary. When I shook his hand, I placed my other hand on his shoulder. Immediately he winced and pulled away in pain, moaning "Owww!"

I didn't intend to hurt him when I greeted him. Actually, I was trying to make him feel loved and accepted. I had gently touched him on his shoulder, the same thing I had done to several other folks that morning. However, no one else had pulled away from me. Why did this man react differently from the rest? I discovered that he'd injured his shoulder a few days before.

Ouch! I had touched his sore spot.

All of a sudden a whole new world unfolded before me as I began to understand how physical injuries can teach us about spiritual wounds. Through this experience I realized why people with wounded spirits react abnormally. They're protecting sore spots on their souls. The slightest touch on their hurting area will send them to the emergency room. Their wounded hearts still ache today, and it affects how they view others.

Even King David had a sore spot. He said, "I am afflicted and needy, and my heart is wounded within me" (Ps. 109:22).

Because a sore spot is invisible, no one knows where it's located until someone touches it. An abnormal reaction to an innocent remark, which wouldn't bother a healthy person, usually indicates a hidden hurt has been detected.

Although we may have been wounded years ago, an unhealed sore spot can still cause pain today. Whenever someone does or says something that triggers a hurtful memory, we flinch and withdraw in pain.

The way we handle our hurts will determine whether we limp through life licking our wounds or allow the Lord to heal our injuries and live victoriously. If our hurts aren't healed, we'll view others through *wounded glasses*.

Damage to our heart creates a lens that perverts the way we see people. Rather than embracing them, we keep them at a distance. We view everyone as a potential attacker who might compound our pain. We're afraid of forming new relationships because we can't stand the thought of being hurt again.

Could it be that you're protecting a wounded heart?

⁓ Wounded Hearts Club

How do I hurt thee? Let me count the ways.

Although we can be injured in countless ways, the following five symptoms indicate that we're still aching from past hurts.

Symptom #1: Being easily injured

Each time a person is touched on a sore spot, the injury becomes a little more sensitive. Wounded people have a very low tolerance for pain, which makes them highly susceptible to being easily injured. Because the man in my church had a previous shoulder injury, a light touch on his sore spot compounded his pain.

I placed my hand on several shoulders that same morning, but none of the others winced or withdrew in pain. Healthy people aren't nursing wounds. A normal touch does not hurt. It takes quite a wallop to hurt a healthy person, but it takes only the slightest touch to send a wounded person reeling. People with unhealed wounds are vulnerable to be injured again and again.

An innocent comment to a wounded individual can trigger the memory of a prior injury. The injured person then responds abnormally to the remark out of his or her wounded memory of the previous hurt. People with sore spots are continually being injured by those *who are completely unaware* they are hurting the individual. The healthy person's words wouldn't hurt another healthy individual; he assumes his statements are harmless. What he doesn't realize is the victim is easily offended even by innocent words. Wounded people are hypersensitive in their area of hurt—all someone has to do is push the wrong button.

One man told me about his continuing arguments with his wife. "She would push my button, and then I would push hers." They took turns hitting each other's sore spots!

In 1997 two men from France lost their lives when they innocently stepped on a bomb that had been dropped during World War I. The shell had been lying dormant for eighty-one years under the battlefield of Verdun. When the men walked on the unsuspecting location and applied pressure on the buried bomb, they set off the explosive device.

The slightest pressure on a sore spot can unleash all the pent-up anger and hostility buried inside. It doesn't matter how many years ago the bomb was buried—the sensitivity remains the same as if the offense happened yesterday. These wounds from the past are land mines implanted deep within. The slightest pressure by others can trigger an explosive reaction.

Symptom #2: Suspicion of others

Wounded glasses program us to view others with suspicion. A dog named Spot had been frequently beaten by its master. One day Spot was wandering down the street when a boy picked up a stick to play fetch with him. When the dog saw him pick up the stick, it took off running with its tail between its legs.

See Spot run.

Although the boy just wanted to play, the dog had been conditioned to associate the stick with pain. The beatings as a puppy programmed Spot to assume that *all* people were out to hurt him.

After we've received a few "beatings" from others, we'll start viewing everyone with suspicion. We assume they have an agenda to hurt us, so we react by running away. Sore spots make us run. Although others may not intend harm, we misjudge their motives because we view them through wounded glasses.

Symptom #3: Difficulty loving others

Wounded people often struggle when it comes to showing love. A person with a toothache has a hard time loving others. Consumed with his or her own pain, the person becomes self-absorbed. All of the person's attention goes to one's own hurt, rather than caring about how others may feel.

It's rare for a wounded soldier in the midst of battle to have the strength and motivation to help another wounded soldier. The soldier's own pain short-circuits his concern for others. A hero might make an effort to help someone else in the same condition, but an injured soldier's greatest need is to get to a hospital. After the wound is healed, he has a much greater ability to show love and concern for others.

> An injured soldier's greatest need is to get to a hospital.

Symptom #4:
Victim mentality

It's easy for a wounded individual to acquire a "victim mentality," not to be confused with a truly innocent victim of abuse. This attitude blames others for every real or imagined offense.

Several years ago a woman pulled into a McDonald's restaurant drive-through and ordered a cup of coffee. As she drove away she slammed on her brakes, spilling the hot coffee onto her lap—causing her to scald herself. The woman sued the McDonald's because of her burn, claiming the injury was their fault. She was awarded $3 million. (Perhaps the jury was composed of people with victim mentalities.)

After this decision, someone suggested that McDonald's needed to print a disclaimer on their cups: "Allow coffee to cool before applying to lap area."

People with victim mentalities go beyond reason in their accusations instead of taking responsibility for their own sins and failures. It's common for a person with a victim mentality to gravitate toward another wounded person so the two "victims" can sympathize with each other. Holding grudges, sulking, finger-pointing, and keeping hurt lists are signs of victim mentality. Trying to restore these people can be a difficult task, because they refuse to acknowledge their own faults. Healing of victim mentality is impossible without true repentance.

Symptom #5: Keeping others at a distance

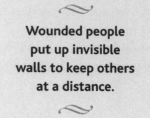

Wounded people put up invisible walls to keep others at a distance.

To prevent future injury, some wounded people put up invisible walls to keep others at a distance. "A brother offended is harder to be won than a strong city, and contentions are like the bars of a castle" (Prov. 18:19).

In ancient times a strong city was characterized by its walls which were constructed as a defense mechanism. A strong city was difficult to capture because of its fortified walls, and its inhabitants constantly defended themselves.

Offended people are hard to befriend because of their defensiveness. They've constructed invisible walls around themselves to keep others from getting close.

I knew a man who had been jilted by a girlfriend. His advice to other men was: "Don't ever trust a woman." He constructed a wall of self-defense around himself, not just to keep his former girlfriend away, but to keep all women out of his life. He avoided close relationships with women because he didn't want to be hurt again. A wounded person will often go to great lengths to avoid encounters with others.

Take Off Your Glasses

Do you have any of the above symptoms? If so, are you ready to take off your glasses? You have to quit replaying your hurt. Three keys are necessary to unlock healing for your internal injuries.

1. The Desperation Key

The first key to recovery is to become desperate. Christ once encountered a blind beggar named Bartimaeus, who cried out for mercy (Mark 10:46-52). Jesus asked him an unusual question: "What do you want Me to do for you?" (v. 51).

What an opportunity—Jesus offered him a blank check. All the blind man had to do was fill in the amount— EYES THAT CAN SEE WITH 20/20 VISION.

Although the answer seemed obvious, He wanted Bartimaeus to be specific in his request. Jesus wanted to see how desperate he was to receive sight. This blind man could have responded by asking for less than what Christ wanted to do for him. He could have asked for a Seeing Eye dog, a new white cane, or a Braille Bible.

He asks the same question of us when we cry out for healing from our past hurts: "What do you want Me to do for you?"

Examine yourself and be honest. Do you really want to be made well?

On another occasion, Jesus was at the pool of Bethesda where He encountered a man who had been on a pallet for thirty-eight years (see John 5:1–9). Jesus asked, "Do you wish to get well?" That's another bizarre question to ask someone who hasn't walked for almost four decades.

Jesus never wasted His words. He asked questions like these to probe the heart. He wanted the lame man to examine himself to find out if he actually wanted to be cured or just wanted sympathy.

Perhaps the crippled man had told others for so many years that he wanted to be healed that his words had no meaning. Maybe he became so dependent on his friends helping him that he didn't want to take responsibility for himself. Over the years many people changed his clothes, carried his pallet, and brought him food.

After Jesus healed him, his first assignment was to pick up his pallet. Christ wanted the formerly lame man to now take responsibility for his own life rather than depend on others to meet his needs.

Unfortunately, many wounded people aren't desperate enough to ask God to heal their hidden hurts. They would rather sulk than be saved. They're more interested in being carried on the pallet of self-pity than receiving a healing touch from the Master's hand.

What is your pallet? Wounds from others? Guilt from an abortion? A life filled with addictions? God wants to use your pallet for a different purpose after you've been healed.

Think of it—your past injury can turn into a powerful testimony of His healing power!

2. The Confession Key

Confession is the second key to recovery. When checking into a hospital, a patient must give the doctor permission to find out what's wrong. The patient can't be healed if he or she keeps pushing the doctor away, trying to guard the injury.

As long as we cover up our sore spot, our injury will continue to fester in darkness. Confession transfers our wound out of the darkness and into the light where Jesus can treat and heal us. As the Scriptures state, "All things become visible when they are exposed by the light" (Eph. 5:13).

Failure to admit the hurt keeps the wound in darkness which provides fertile soil for the root of bitterness to grow. The writer of Hebrews warns about this dangerous attitude: "See to it that no one comes short of the grace of God; that no root of bitterness springing up causes trouble, and by it many be defiled" (Heb. 12:15).

Bitterness is the offspring of an unhealed wound—whose parents are unforgivingness and time. The longer you allow the root of bitterness to grow in the soil of your heart, the more love it will devour. Eventually it will consume all the love in your heart unless you repent.

Healing begins the moment
you expose your wound to the
light. Confession means to admit
you've wrongly held on to your
hurt. James says to, "Confess
your sins to one another, and
pray for one another so that
you may be healed" (James
5:16).

> The longer we allow
> the root of bitter-
> ness to grow in our
> hearts, the more love
> it will devour.

3. The Forgiveness Key

Forgiving those who have hurt you is the third key to recovery. Unwillingness to forgive is the number one barrier that
shuts down healing. Unforgivingness is the primary reason
why sore spots never heal in the first place. Unconditional forgiveness when an offense occurs can prevent a hidden hurt
from forming.

If you truly want to be healed, you must stop wishing evil
to come upon those who have offended you. God rushes to the
aid of those who forgive without reservation.

For years Laura was mentally, physically, and emotionally
abused by her husband. Later he was committed into a mental institution after several attempts to kill her. They divorced
shortly thereafter and went their separate ways.

Twenty years later, Laura faced and overcame a drinking
problem. She found needed help by attending support group
meetings. During one of the discussions at the group meeting
another member of the support group rudely confronted her.
This man spoke to her in the same abusive tone of voice as her
former husband. Immediately it brought back all the old feelings of unworthiness, shame, and guilt from her relationship
over two decades prior to this.

Ouch! He touched a sore spot. When he touched her injury, she glared at him through her wounded glasses and envisioned her former spouse yelling at her. She argued with the man just like she had with her ex-husband and then stormed out the door. For two weeks she was angry—

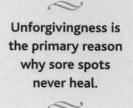

Unforgivingness is the primary reason why sore spots never heal.

not with the man from the support group—but with her former husband. The man from the support group had touched her sore spot, which called up the painful memories from years before.

Laura realized she had carried that hurt long enough. Twenty years had passed and the injury was still controlling her. If time could heal wounds, twenty years would have done it. It takes more than time to heal sore spots. The balm of forgiveness must be applied to the infected area.

Laura got down on her knees and forgave her former husband for his abusive behavior. Then she asked God to forgive her of the bitterness she had been harboring. At the next meeting she asked forgiveness from the man at the support group.

Through her decision to forgive, God miraculously cured her wounded heart. Peace filled her soul for the first time in years. No longer would she view others through wounded glasses. Laura isn't haunted anymore by the hurtful memories from an abusive past.

Ahhh . . . sore spot healed.

Can't happen to you, you say?

Yes, it can. You can be set free from your prison of hurt. Just use the keys.

TEN

Bitterness Glasses: Snake Bites

Forgiveness is surrendering my right to hurt you for hurting me.

~ ARCHIBALD HART

IN 1996 Valentin Grimaldo was walking along U.S. Highway 281 in south Texas. He reached down into a clump of grass to pick up something when a poisonous coral snake bit him on the hand. Grimaldo bit off the snake's head, skinned it, and used the skin as a tourniquet to keep the venom from spreading.[1] His quick thinking saved his life.

A similar incident happened to the apostle Paul on his way to Rome. He had just survived a shipwreck that stranded the passengers on an island called Malta. The natives welcomed them and built a fire to warm their weary guests. Paul was reaching down to place a stick on the fire when a viper slithered out of the woodpile and fastened itself to his hand.

First nearly killed at sea. Now bitten by a deadly snake. Just when he thinks he's out of dangerous waters, the snakes come out of the woodwork. Did he blame the natives for not snake-proofing the campsite?

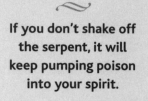

If you don't shake off the serpent, it will keep pumping poison into your spirit.

No. He shook it off into the fire (Acts 28:5). Apparently Paul didn't believe in snake handling.

On our voyage through life, we're going to receive some snake bites. Not from coral snakes or vipers. I'm talking about spiritual snakebites. Satan is a serpent, and he wants to attach himself to our spirits so that he can inject his venom.

When the snake bites, we can either let it hang on—or we can shake it off. If we don't shake off the serpent, it will continue to pump poison into our spirits. And that's how people become bitter.

When our attitude becomes poisoned, we start looking at others differently. *Bitterness glasses* make us view those we dislike in venomous ways. That's why we need to forgive every person who has hurt us.

Peter's Little Black Book

Peter once asked Jesus, "Lord, how often shall my brother sin against me and I forgive him? Up to seven times?" (Matt. 18:21).

I have a sneaking suspicion that Peter had someone in mind, maybe Thomas.

Thomas mocked me when I tried to walk on water. That's one.

I stubbed my toe and Thomas didn't pray for me. I've noticed he's become insensitive to my needs lately. That's two.

Thomas and Andrew went fishing last week without me. That's three.

When Peter had eight offenses logged in his little black book, he asked Jesus if he could stop forgiving after seven times.

Jesus answered, "I don't say to you, up to the seventh time, but *every* time—Peter, when the snake bites, shake it off!"

"OK, Jesus. But—uh—can I still call You 'Lord' if I refuse to forgive?"

Many people today call Jesus "Lord" while holding unforgivingness in their hearts. It's been a problem for centuries. Even in Jesus' day, He rebuked them for this hypocrisy by saying, "Why do you call Me, 'Lord, Lord,' and do not do what I say?" (Luke 6:46).

What did He say? He said to forgive everyone every time. Jesus taught His disciples to pray, "Forgive us our debts, as we also have forgiven our debtors" (Matt. 6:12). Although many people love to recite the Lord's Prayer, not many love to forgive their debtors. So they edit the Lord's Prayer, changing the parts they don't like.

The Lord's Prayer, RSV (Revised Several Verses)

Our Father who art in heaven, hallowed be Thy name.
Thy kingdom come. Thy will be done, on earth as it is
    in heaven.
Give us this day our daily bread.
And forgive us our debts . . .*
And do not lead us into temptation†
But deliver us from evil††
For Thine is the kingdom, and the power, and the glory,
    forever. Amen.

* Deleted from original prayer: "as we also have forgiven our debtors"
† Except when we *want* to be tempted
†† Only the scary kind of evil

C. S. Lewis said, "Everyone says forgiveness is a lovely idea until they have to forgive someone."

Forgiveness isn't optional—it's essential. Forgiveness doesn't operate only when we feel good. It's an act of our will when we don't feel like doing it.

Forgiveness isn't a onetime event. It's a never-ending process. Jesus said to keep extending mercy to those who have hurt us. Each day brings new offenses, requiring new forgiveness. Every time we're offended, we must forgive. No exceptions.

It's for our own good. Forgiveness prevents bitterness from poisoning our heart. If we don't forgive, we allow the snake to inject its venom into our spirit. Just as the serpent lied to Adam and Eve, he wants to tell us a few fibs as well. He speaks to our minds, trying to keep us from forgiving others.

Bitterness is a process, which takes place in four stages.

Stage 1: Offense

Someone offends us. A so-called friend betrays us. A colleague makes a devastating comment about us. A family member wrongfully judges us. And it hurts! The serpent plants this thought in our minds: *I'm offended by what he [she] did to me.*

> Every bitter person had his or her start through being offended by someone.

Offenses can be real or imagined. While some people intentionally hurt us, others don't mean to. Although their actions may be innocent, we get offended through our imaginations and assumptions.

When someone hurts our feelings, Satan tempts us to become resentful. Every bitter person had his or her start through being offended by someone. He or she *chose* to be offended. We must act immediately during the offense stage to forgive the offender. If we shake it off, we'll maintain our spiritual freedom and joy. If we don't, we proceed to stage 2.

Stage 2: Anger

If we hold on to the offense rather than shake it off, the hurt turns into anger. The devil plants another thought: *I'm still mad at what he [she] did to me!*

Anger comes in many shapes and sizes. Things don't go the way we like and we get angry. Our teenager won't clean her room, so we get mad. Our spouse goes out and buys something we can't afford and this makes us boil inside.

Ephesians 4:26 says, "Do not let the sun go down on your anger." That means we must get rid of our rage before the day is over. We must deliberately choose to forgive the offender and move on. If we don't resolve our wrath by the next day, our anger will degenerate into resentment.

Stage 3: Unforgivingness

Unforgivingness is prolonged anger and resentment. It drains the love out of our hearts so that we view others with scorn. Satan makes another suggestion: *I just can't forgive right now. Maybe later.*

I've been hearing a lot lately about "hate crimes." Call me naïve if you will, but I've never heard of a "love crime." Refusing to forgive is a hate crime. It's a crime in God's eyes to not forgive.

You've heard the expression "Hate the sin; love the sinner." As a husband and wife were leaving church, the husband said, "Just between you and me, I hate the sinners as much as I hate the sins."

Just between you and me, let's call unforgivingness what it really is—hatred. We don't like to think of our unforgiving-

ness as hatred because we want
to justify our ungodly attitudes.
We secretly desire to see our
enemies punished, then wash
our hands of the guilt like
pompous Pontius Pilates.

> Let's call unforgiv-
> ingness what it
> really is—hatred.

Sigmund Freud once said,
"We must forgive our enemies,
but not before they have been
hanged." When we don't forgive, we want justice administered
to our enemies instead of mercy.

Bible teacher Warren Wiersbe said one of the most miserable men he ever met kept a notebook listing the people who
had offended him. Whenever someone did something he
didn't like, he wrote it down on his hurt list. The book was
filled with names and offenses.[2]

We may not record our hurts in a journal, but do we jot
them down in our mental notebooks? Whenever we don't forgive, we chronicle each crime in our cerebral diaries. As we write
about others in our books, God is writing about us in His book.
First Corinthians 13:5 says love does not take into account a
wrong suffered. That means we must tear up our "hurt list."

Step 4: Bitterness

As unforgivingness continues to fester, the infection of bitterness oozes into our hearts. The devil says, *I can't stand that guy.
I'll never forgive him.* Bitterness is a spiritual ulcer, which is the
result of an unhealed wound. At this stage, our spirits have
become poisoned, causing us to view others with hatred.

Several years ago after an elderly woman passed away, family members were cleaning out her house when they found a
scrapbook filled with obituaries from the local newspaper.
Many of the death notices pertained to people she had detested.

As bizarre as it may sound, she kept a scrapbook of her dead enemies.

This woman had five different clippings of her most despised foe in her morbid memory book. Apparently she had gained some kind of strange satisfaction by thinking they could no longer torment her. Or could they? If we don't forgive our deceased enemies, they'll continue to haunt us through our hateful memories of them.

Few people escape once they reach stage four. Because bitter people stay offended and angry, they remain trapped inside the dungeon of their own making. Only through radical repentance can these prisoners be set free.

〜 Take Off Your Glasses

These are probably the most difficult of all glasses to remove. Bitterness creates a stronghold that takes over a person's spirit like a cancer. Only by the grace of God through forgiveness can an individual be set free from this distorted way of viewing others. Here are the steps required to take off these bitterness glasses.

1. Shake it off.

Jesus said, "You have heard that it was said, 'An eye for an eye, and a tooth for a tooth.' But I say to you, do not resist an evil person; but whoever slaps you on your right cheek, turn the other to him also" (Matt. 5:38, 39).

Don't resist him who is evil? Mr. Logic tells me that we *should* resist evil. Although it doesn't seem to make sense, Jesus specifically commanded us to not resist those who offend us.

When the snake strikes, don't strike back. We must not pick up the weapon of hate and retaliate against our enemies. "Never pay back evil for evil to anyone" (Rom. 12:17). Returning evil for evil is the first step in the bitterness process. Instead of fighting back, shake it off.

When Paul shook off the snake, he suffered no harm. If you'll learn to shake off offenses, you won't be harmed either. Things that used to bug you won't bother you anymore. You must not give the snake the slightest opportunity to poison your spirit.

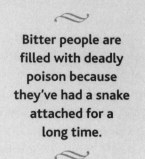

Bitter people are filled with deadly poison because they've had a snake attached for a long time.

Bitter people are filled with deadly poison because they've had a snake attached for a long time. It's a case of hate at first bite. Their spirits are full of venom because they didn't shake it off when the snake first struck. As long as the snake is still attached, it will keep injecting venom. The longer you let it hang on, the more poison will fill your heart.

2. Let go of offenses.

A man named Simon wanted to buy the Holy Spirit with money. Peter told him, "Your heart is not right before God.... For I see that you are in the gall of bitterness and in the bondage of iniquity" (Acts 8:21–23). The Greek word *gall* means "poison." Peter could see that Simon was wearing bitterness glasses, which imprisoned him in spiritual bondage. Bitterness not only poisons our spirit but also handcuffs us in the bondage of iniquity.

Natives in Africa capture monkeys by setting up cages and placing bait inside. The bait can be anything a monkey would want, such as food or an unusual object. The monkeys are lured to the cages but are too smart to actually go inside. Instead, they reach through the bars, grab the bait, and try to pull it out. Because the object is too large to go through the bars, the only way the monkey can get away is to drop the bait. But monkeys refuse to let go. They kick and squeal but keep holding on. They stay trapped in bondage because they refuse to let go of the bait.

Are you the devil's monkey? Have you grabbed Satan's bait, which is called *offenses?* Satan sets his trap, using offenses as bait. If you grab the offense, you will be his prisoner as long as you hold on. Many people are incarcerated in the devil's dungeon because they refuse to let go. You must choose to let go of all past offenses and keep your hands off all future ones.

3. Be an instant forgiver.

Bitter people need to get the venom out of their spiritual bloodstreams. Love is the anti-venom for hatred, and forgiveness is the serum for the poison of bitterness. "Let all bitterness and wrath and anger and clamor and slander be put away from you, along with all malice. Be kind to one another, tenderhearted, forgiving each other, just as God in Christ also has forgiven you" (Eph. 4:31, 32). When you let Christ's love and forgiveness fill your heart, the poison of bitterness will be neutralized.

In the book of Acts, Stephen hadn't done anything wrong when his persecutors stoned him. All he did was preach a message about Israeli history. The congregation didn't like his sermon that day, so they picked up rocks and cast their votes. Even as he was being stoned, Stephen prayed that God would forgive his attackers (see Acts 7:54–60).

Praying for his enemies as he was being stoned? Why?

Stephen was an *instant forgiver.*

Bitter people won't forgive when they're offended. They hold on to their hurts while the serpent pumps his poison into their spirits.

Stephen was about to die and within a matter of seconds would stand face-to-face with God Almighty. He didn't want to face his Creator with unforgivingness in his heart. So as his persecutors stoned him, he cried out for God to forgive them. (If you were to die today and stand before God, would you be holding any grudges?)

Heaven opened up, and Stephen saw Jesus standing at the right hand of God (see Acts 7:56). Other verses in the Bible refer to Jesus *seated* at the right hand of God. I would like to think that Jesus was giving Stephen a standing ovation for forgiving those who killed him. No matter what others did to him, Stephen graciously extended mercy to his enemies.

For several years an Olathe, Kansas, lawyer has done something almost unheard-of in the legal profession. At Christmas he forgives past-due bills of $5,000 to $10,000 owed by his clients. Two insights led him to do this.

First, he realized that debt creates bondage and that God intends forgiveness to be material as well as spiritual. Second, he realized unpaid debts produced resentment in his life. He discovered the way to free himself from bondage was to forgive. His first experience of forgiving the debts felt so good that he decided to continue the practice.

Prior to Christmas each year, he writes a letter to clients who haven't paid their bills in several months. The letter reads,

> Your bill, a copy which is enclosed, is hereby forgiven in its entirety. In exchange for forgiving your debt I would ask two things of you if I could. First, would you forgive me if I have offended you? Second, would you during the next month forgive at least one person who owes you money or has offended you? Have a most blessed Christmas.[3]

Some things are more valuable than money—like peace of mind and a joyful heart.

Jesus taught this same principle in the parable of the unmerciful slave. The king forgave his slave a $50 million debt and simply wanted him to forgive all his own debtors in return (Matt. 18:23–35).

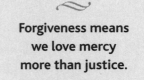

Forgiveness means we love mercy more than justice.

The King of the universe has forgiven your $50 million spiritual debt. All He asks is for you to forgive those who have offended you. Are you willing to do that?

When your heart overflows with compassion, it's not hard to show mercy to those who have hurt you. God wants you to do justice but to *love* mercy (Mic. 6:8). Justice is good, but mercy is better. Forgiveness means you love mercy more than justice.

Showing mercy to your enemies shatters the lenses of bitterness. Then you'll see as God sees.

ELEVEN

Judgmental Glasses: The Speck Inspectors

Always listen to a man when he describes the faults of others. Ofttimes, most times, he's describing his own, revealing himself.

~MALCOLM FORBES

A FATHER, SON, and their donkey were traveling from one village to another. The boy walked while the man rode the donkey. The father overheard a bystander say, "That's a shame. Look how that man is making that poor boy walk."

Not wanting to be the object of criticism, the father and son changed places. The boy rode the donkey while the man walked. He then heard a woman comment, "Look how that boy on the donkey is making that poor man walk."

The father and son both climbed onto the donkey. As they traveled down the road, someone said, "Look how that man and boy are making that poor donkey suffer."

They both got off and walked. The people remarked, "Look at that stupid man and boy. They're walking when they could be riding that donkey."

When they entered the next village, the boy was walking and the man was carrying the donkey.

No matter what we do, someone will find fault. People wearing *judgmental glasses* overlook their own faults to criticize others. Jesus said,

> Why do you look at the speck that is in your brother's eye, but do not notice the log that is in your own eye? Or how can you say to your brother, "Let me take the speck out of your eye," and behold, the log is in your own eye? You hypocrite, first take the log out of your own eye, and then you will see clearly to take the speck out of your brother's eye (Matt. 7:3–5).

⟿ Here Comes the Judge

A person wearing judgmental glasses inspects for specks in others and thinks he is always right. "The way of a fool is right in his own eyes" (Prov. 12:15). The Pharisees viewed Jesus through judgmental glasses, trying to find fault with the perfect Son of God. "The scribes and the Pharisees were watching Him closely . . . so that they might find reason to accuse Him" (Luke 6:7). Their warped perspective made them fabricate imperfections, even though He was sinless.

These are some of the most popular glasses worn today. I would like to introduce you to a few speck inspectors.

Perfectionist Pete. Quick on the flaw. Judges every mistake a person makes. No one can ever reach his unattainable expectations, including himself.

Sarcastic Sally. Cuts others down to make herself look better. Criticizes by using snide remarks.

Teasing Tom. Makes jabs by joking. Rips others apart under the guise of humor. Excuses himself by saying, "Can't you take a joke?"

Gossiping Gilda. Loves to talk about people behind their backs but not to their faces. Blabs about others' faults, exaggerating each one.

Angry Allen. An "in-your-face" kind of guy. His internal anger boils over with criticism. Reprimands people face-to-face and doesn't care how it devastates them.

Preying Pamela. Exposes others' faults through prayer requests. She preys instead of prays. "We need to pray for Marlene. I think she might be pregnant and doesn't know who the father is."

Jealous Julia. Feels threatened by other women. Points out their imperfections in an attempt to make her rivals look ugly.

Grumpy Greg. Doesn't like himself. Likes others even less. Never has an uplifting word proceeding from his mouth.

Judging is what we see. Criticism is what we say. Critical people always make derogatory comments about others. They slip on judgmental glasses and start inspecting for faults. As they dissect others, they speak volumes about themselves. It has been said, "Great people talk about ideas, mediocre people talk about things, little people talk about other people." To belittle is to be little.

To belittle is to be little.

The biblical term for "criticize" is "curse." To *bless* someone means "to speak well of" another person. Old Testament patriarchs would bless their children, extending their wishes for their well-being. When we bless others, we desire God's best for them.

To *curse* means "to speak evil of," wishing harm upon another. Cursing describes a person in an attacking way rather than a redemptive way. When we make critical comments about others, we curse them by assaulting their character.

The tongue can be used to bring either blessing or cursing:

> With it we bless our Lord and Father, and with it we curse men, who have been made in the likeness of God; from the same mouth come both blessing and cursing. My brethren, these things ought not to be this way. Does a fountain send out from the same opening both fresh and bitter water? (James 3:9–11).

The apostle James tells us that it's wrong to bless the Creator and then curse His creation. That's like praising a particular artist to his face and then making fun of his paintings behind his back. We adore our Creator by speaking about others in a respectful way. Even when others persecute us, we must bless them and not retaliate with hateful words. "Bless those who persecute you; bless and do not curse" (Rom. 12:14).

The apostle Paul once called Ananias the high priest a "whitewashed wall" (Acts 23:3). He then apologized for his remarks. "I was not aware, brethren, that he was high priest; for it is written, 'YOU SHALL NOT SPEAK EVIL OF A RULER OF YOUR PEOPLE'" (Acts 23:5).

God doesn't want us to curse those who rule us. Although we might disagree with their policies, we need to pray for them, not curse them. If we need to correct someone, we can speak the truth in love

> Critical people always make derogatory comments about others.

without being critical of that individual. We can reprove and rebuke without cursing (2 Tim. 4:2). The line is drawn inside our hearts. What are our motives? Could we say it if Jesus were present and listening?

∿ Critic's Choice

Critics choose to see people's faults because of a bigger flaw within themselves. Jesus said speck inspectors have logs in their own eyes. The following reasons explain why people find fault.

Judgmental people have lost their compassion for others.

A man wrote love letters to his fiancée, a schoolteacher. She sent the letters back with the spelling and vocabulary corrected.

> ∿
> **As compassion decreases, criticism increases.**
> ∿

If we're only looking for mistakes, we will miss the love message others are trying to send. Like oil and water, love and criticism can't intermingle.

People who look through judgmental glasses have lost their compassion. They view others maliciously because their love is depleted. The degree of judging others is inversely proportional to the amount of mercy in their hearts. The greater their judgment, the less their love. As their compassion decreases, their criticism increases.

Judgmental people have the same faults as the ones they judge.

> You have no excuse, everyone of you who passes judgment, for in that which you judge another, you condemn yourselves;

for you who judge practice the same things. . . . But do you
suppose this, O man, when you pass judgment on those
who practice such things and do the same yourselves, that
you will escape the judgment of God? (Rom. 2:1, 3).

When we drive down the highway, we naturally notice vehicles that look exactly like our own. Although hundreds of other
cars might be on the freeway, our eyes are drawn to the copies
of ours. A little picture of our own car is embedded in our
brain, which becomes a magnet for drawing our attention.

In the same way, judgmental people are familiar with their
own faults, and their eyes are naturally drawn to similar sins
in others. Paul wrote pointedly, "You who preach that one
should not steal, do you steal?" (Rom. 2:21). Faultfinders
harshly describe the flaws they see in others, but never
acknowledge that they themselves commit those same sins.

A man and his wife pulled into a gas station to refuel their
car. As the tank was being refilled, the station attendant
washed the windshield. When he finished, the driver said, "The
windshield is still dirty. Wash it again."

"Yes, sir," the attendant answered. He scrubbed the windshield a second time, looking closely for any bugs or dirt he
might have missed. When he finished, the man in the car
became angry.

"It's still dirty!" he yelled. "Don't you know how to wash a
windshield? Do it again."

The attendant cleaned the windshield a third time, carefully looking for anyplace he might have missed but finding
no messy spots anywhere. By now the driver was fuming. He
screamed, "This windshield is still filthy! I'm going to talk to
your boss to make sure you don't work here another day!
You're the worst windshield washer I've ever seen!"

As he was about to get out of the car, his wife reached over
and removed his glasses. She carefully wiped them with a tis-

sue and then put them back on him. The driver embarrassingly slumped down into his seat as he observed a spotless windshield.[1]

Critical people see others' faults because they look through dirty judgmental glasses. They criticize what they perceive to be dirt on others when in reality they look through the filth on their own hearts.

Judgmental people form opinions based on partial or misleading information.

A friend of mine sells tires. One day he received a call from an unsatisfied customer. "You sold me a couple of defective tires," the man griped. "The whitewalls are peeling off, and I want you to replace them free of charge."

"Let me guess," my friend said. "Are the front and back tires on the passenger side the ones peeling?"

"As a matter of fact, yes—they are. How did you know?" the surprised customer answered.

"They're tearing up because when you parallel park, you pull too close to the curb and rub your tires against the concrete," my friend replied. "That's why the whitewalls are peeling off."

The customer criticized the salesman because he had overlooked one important piece of information—the culprit was himself! After he discovered that he had caused his own problem, he had nothing more to say.

A judgmental person makes assessments without having all the facts. Because critical people don't know the whole story, they form unfavorable opinions based on incomplete information.

A football coach pulls his quarterback out of the game. Spectators in the stands slip on judgmental glasses and criticize their coach, not realizing that the player has been injured.

They make harsh judgments against the coach because they're ignorant of the quarterback's inability to play.

Employers don't have the time to explain to every employee the factors they must consider in running their companies. Yet laborers criticize their bosses' decisions because they see only a small piece of the puzzle.

Some parishioners are quick to make judgments about their pastors based on partial information. Godly ministers often receive undeserved criticism due to unrealistic expectations. Most church members don't understand what it's like to live in a glass house with no privacy. They don't know about the numerous counseling phone calls ministers receive at home, even in the middle of the night. The ministry has one of the highest rates for burnout of any profession, partly because judgmental parishioners make life hard on their pastors. If the roles were reversed, the critics would view things quite differently.

It's easy to judge when we don't understand. A familiar old proverb says, "Never criticize a man until you've walked a mile in his moccasins." We won't know the whole story about the one we criticize until we've walked in her shoes or felt the load on his back.

⟿ Take Off Your Glasses

Do you understand how your criticism grieves the Lord? You can make the world a kinder, gentler place to live in by taking off your judgmental glasses.

1. Take the log out of your own eye.

The logs in your eyes are the judgmental glasses you look through. Jesus explained how to clear up your vision: "First take the log out of your own eye, and then you will see clearly to take the speck out of your brother's eye" (Matt. 7:5).

You can remove the tree in your eye by correcting your own faults. First, repent of your critical attitude. Are you unfair in your assessments? Do you have selfish motives, or are you biased in your opinions? Remember that God will judge you in the way you judge others. "In the way you judge, you will be judged; and by your standard of measure, it will be measured to you" (Matt. 7:2).

Second, repent of the sins that you judge in others. If you do an internal inspection, you may very well discover the same problems within yourselves. When your heart is cleansed, the logs will fall out of your eyes, and your judgmental opinions will cease.

2. Change the way you talk about others.

The best indicator of what resides in your heart is the way you talk about others. *Gossip* is what you say behind someone's back but would never say to his or her face. "He who goes about as a slanderer reveals secrets, therefore do not associate with a gossip" (Prov. 20:19). *Flattery* is what you say to a person's face but would never say behind his or her back. "They speak falsehood to one another; with flattering lips and with a double heart they speak" (Ps. 12:2). Both gossip and flattery are symptoms of a polluted heart.

A repentant heart will alter the way you view people. As your perspective adjusts, how you talk about others will also change. "The mouth speaks out of that which fills the heart" (Matt. 12:34). You speak blessing rather than cursing. Instead of looking for the specks, look for the spectacular. When you remove your judgmental glasses, you'll be amazed at how much good you find in others.

3. Show mercy instead of judgment.

As compassion increases, criticism decreases.

Everyone has shortcomings—including you. If you want mercy from God, you must show mercy to others. "Judgment will be merciless to one who has shown no mercy; mercy triumphs over judgment" (James 2:13). Judgment is quick to find faults, but mercy will overlook imperfections. "Above all, keep fervent in your love for one another, because love covers a multitude of sins" (1 Pet. 4:8). As your compassion increases, your criticism will decrease.

Give the guy a break. He has enough problems without having to endure your criticism. Lift off the curse that you've placed on him. Instead of picking him apart with harsh comments, intercede for him. Ask God to change him from within.

If you'll pray for him instead of prey upon him, God will bestow His blessing upon you. "Blessed are the merciful, for they shall receive mercy" (Matt. 5:7).

Mercy is what I want to receive from the Lord. Especially on Judgment Day.

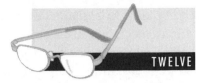

TWELVE

Lust Glasses:
Trouble Vision

Don't mistake pleasure for happiness. They're a different breed of dog.

~ JOSH BILLINGS

*D*OUBLE VISION: Diplopia; a vision disorder in which a single object appears double.

Trouble vision: Lust; a visual problem that leads to the ruin of spiritual health; the source of sexual addictions; a frequent cause of marital trouble.

When the Commission on Pornography testified before a United States Senate committee, one of the members was asked to define pornography. He said, "I don't know how to define it, but I know it when I see it."

Jesus said, "I say to you that everyone who looks at a woman with lust for her has already committed adultery with her in his heart" (Matt. 5:28). A man viewing a woman through *lust glasses* commits the act in his heart.

When Christ made this revelation, most women clothed themselves modestly. They didn't have cosmetics, surgeries, shampoos, perfumes, and a wide variety of revealing clothes as we do today. Although we live in a much different world than two thousand years ago, Christ's statement still holds true.

Your eyes can get you into trouble—deep trouble.

Looking through lust glasses can lead to sexual impurity, unwanted pregnancies, adultery, sexually transmitted diseases, divorce, regrets, and countless heartaches.

Jesus' declaration is especially pertinent when we consider the availability of pornography through movies, magazines, the Internet, and television. We're exposed to porn wherever we go or so it seems. From the convenience store to our own television sets, it confronts us even when we're not looking for it.

⟿ Feeding the Fire

The word *lust* means "strong desire." There's nothing wrong with desires that are fulfilled in God's way. The problem starts when we try to fulfill those needs in ungodly ways. Author Peter Lord has said, "Temptation is trying to fulfill a legitimate, God-given desire in an illegitimate way."

When our desires are misdirected, the trouble begins. Lust leads us on a leash into temptation. "Each one is tempted when he is carried away and enticed by his own lust" (James 1:14).

Being attracted to another person isn't the proof of love. Don't confuse being "in love" with being "in lust." A pastor told me about a young couple who fell madly in lust with each other. He said, "They aren't in love—they're in heat!"

If we want to get out of heat, we must quit feeding the fire. Our sex drive is like a fire that's burning within us. Whenever a person looks at porn, that person is throwing more logs onto the fire, and the flame grows. The more firewood they add, the more they heat up.

It doesn't take long before the sex drive is burning out of control, demanding even more uncensored material. The lust isn't being fulfilled because "the eye is not satisfied with seeing" (Eccles. 1:8). Like an alcoholic, a person becomes addicted. Pornography now rules his or her life.

It's no secret that lust often operates in a secret world. It hides behind closed doors, assuming no one will know, thinking it will never get caught.

Years ago, one of the players on the Dallas Cowboys football team became a Christian. Several months later when the team was in Philadelphia to play the Eagles, a couple of players on the team paid a call girl to tempt the Christian. They gave her a hundred dollars and said, "If you can get that guy to go to bed with you this weekend, we'll double it, and you can have anything he gives you."

The Christian football player didn't know it was a trap. Even so, he didn't yield to the temptation, though it looked as if no one would know. Later he said, "I didn't know what was coming off, but they were watching me. They would have ripped me apart if I had gone to bed with that girl."[1]

Who will ever know?

God will know. You will know. Eventually, the word will leak out, and others will know. On Judgment Day everyone will know. "Nothing is hidden, except to be revealed; nor has anything been secret, but that it would come to light" (Mark 4:22). There's no such thing as a secret life.

To break free from sexual addiction, a person must become *disgusted with their destructive behavior*. We must be more desperate to please God than to satisfy our own desires. Repentance

> Repentance is a decision to want freedom more than bondage.

is a decision to want freedom more than bondage. Without a genuine change of heart, we'll keep returning to the same bad habits. "As a dog returns to his own vomit, so a fool repeats his folly" (Prov. 26:11, NKJV).

∽ Take Off Your Glasses

The Bible instructs us to "keep oneself unstained by the world" (James 1:27). The world is constantly trying to stain us with its filth. To keep spiritually pure, we must take certain preventative measures. The solution is the same now as it has always been. "How can a young man keep his way pure? By keeping it according to Your word" (Ps. 119:9).

Here are some important words of advice that will keep your eyes from getting you into trouble.

1. Love God first and foremost.

Jesus quoted the greatest commandment, "You shall love the Lord your God with all your heart, and with all your soul, and with all your mind" (Matt. 22:37). I can understand how to love the Lord with my heart and soul, but how do I love God with my mind? By controlling the thoughts that enter it. I refuse to let certain thoughts in. I control what my eyes will and will not see.

Many people try to overcome the lust of the flesh by using the strength of the flesh. They try to stop actions, but the desire still resides in their hearts. They keep failing because "the flesh is weak" (Mark 14:38). The flesh, which is our

> ∽
>
> **The only way to overcome lust is through a genuine work of the Holy Spirit in our hearts.**
>
> ∽

natural impulses, cannot overcome the flesh. The very thing that got us into the temptation is now trying to get us out of it!

The Spirit and the flesh are in opposition to one another. "The flesh sets its desire against the Spirit, and the Spirit against the flesh; for *these are in opposition to one another,* so that you may not do the things that you please" (Gal. 5:17, author's emphasis). These desires pull us in opposite directions. We have to decide which will rule our lives—the flesh or Spirit.

The only way to overcome lust is through a genuine work of the Holy Spirit in our hearts. Without a doubt, the most important key to victory over lust is the power of the Spirit. The Holy Spirit is our *only* source for holiness, empowering us to live a godly life. The desires of Spirit will dislodge the lusts of our flesh.

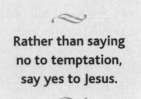

Rather than saying no to temptation, say yes to Jesus.

The apostle Paul wrote, "Walk in the Spirit, and you shall not fulfill the lust of the flesh" (Gal. 5:16, NKJV). Rather than saying no to temptation, say yes to Jesus.

A college student went to a Bible study and became convicted about the pornographic pictures he had pinned up in his room. He went back to his dorm room, posted a picture of Jesus on his wall, and removed the dirty photos.

A friend walked into his room and asked, "What happened to all the pictures on your wall?"

"When I put up the picture of Jesus," he replied, "the other pictures had to go."

How do you walk in the Spirit? By yielding to His leading. Give Him first place in your heart. Give Him the first part of your day by spending time with Him. Read the Bible and talk with Him. Give Him the first part of your income. If you love God more than your money, He will receive the first tenth of what you earn. As you go through the day, seek to please Him in all you do. All these actions are the product of putting God first.

2. Cut off opportunities.

Why do some people have more temptations than others? Simple. They expose themselves to more temptations. "Beloved, I urge you as aliens and strangers to abstain from fleshly lusts which wage war against the soul" (1 Pet. 2:11).

Do the math. The more temptations you expose yourself to, the more battles you'll have to fight. You can reduce your temptations by cutting off opportunities *ahead of time.*

Jesus said, "Keep watching and praying, that you may not enter into temptation; the spirit is willing, but the flesh is weak" (Matt. 26:41). Following this instruction will keep you from entering forbidden areas. Watching keeps you alert to trap doors. Praying keeps your spirit in tune with the Holy Spirit.

Victory comes by taking preventative measures. "Put on the Lord Jesus Christ, and make *no provision* for the flesh in regard to its lusts" (Rom. 13:14, author's emphasis).

Trochilus, one of the disciples of Plato, almost drowned when his ship sank during a storm at sea. When he got back home, the first thing he did was board up the windows that looked out to the sea. He was afraid that on a beautiful day when the ocean was calm, he would be tempted to venture out on another voyage.[2]

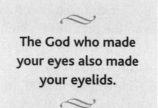

The God who made your eyes also made your eyelids.

Board up your windows. Cut off all opportunities. "Do not give the devil an opportunity" (Eph. 4:27). If you give Satan an inch, he'll become the ruler of your life.

> Just don't go there.

The God who made your eyes also made your eyelids. Job said, "I have made a covenant with my eyes. How then could I gaze at a virgin?" (Job 31:1). You *can* close your eyes to certain things. Use self-control.

If you struggle with lust, "just don't go there." Determine ahead of time that you won't go to certain places. Don't go to porn sites on the Internet. Disconnect your cable TV if that causes you trouble. Just don't go there.

Don't go near places that will make you stumble. "Keep your way far from her [the adulteress] and do not go near the door of her house" (Prov. 5:8). Stay away from stores that sell pornography. Just don't go there. Stop feeding the fire.

I once counseled a man who had a weakness for watching pornographic movies in his motel room when he went on business trips. I told him he needed to use self-control instead of the remote control. If he never turned on the television set, he couldn't be tempted by it. I advised him to forget the TV, but instead take Christian books and his Bible to read.

It worked. He made a plan before he arrived at the motel to replace television watching with book reading. By keeping his mind occupied, he conquered the temptation.

You can remove lust glasses by doing several things: Reduce the time you watch television. Block those television stations that show sexual content by calling your cable company. Don't allow those stations into your home. Quit channel surfing because that increases your chances of coming across something you shouldn't be watching. Put a filter on your Internet browser that blocks the sites containing sexual content.

If you still have a problem, disconnect your satellite receiver, cable television, and Internet service. You must purposely prevent temptation, or it will come looking for you.

> Use self-control instead of the remote control.

Do you see what I mean? If you don't go there, you win. For every opportunity you cut off, that's one less battle you have to fight, which is a guaranteed victory.

3. Fast and pray.

Author and speaker Kay Arthur has said, "Every desire we have will either be killed or fulfilled." When persons quit feeding their lust, their appetite for sex will decrease. "For lack of wood the fire goes out" (Prov. 26:20). Their mind will clear up. Eventually they'll discover that they can go days without ever thinking about looking at pornography. The desires that once controlled their minds have been starved.

No one will ever forget January 28, 1986, when the space shuttle *Challenger* exploded before the world's eyes. The trail of the solid rocket boosters could be seen careening in the sky out of control. When a rocket is under control, it performs a beneficial purpose. Out of control, it caused destruction.

When desires are under God's control, they're good and legitimate. But when out of control, they become destructive addictions.

Ted Haggard, pastor of New Life Church in Colorado Springs, counsels sex addicts with a unique technique. He puts them on a fast. Fasting means to go without food while praying. Addictions are drives that have gotten out of control, and a fast starves the appetites so they can come back to their proper place.

As you take charge over your hunger drive, your sex drive will also come under control. This isn't a diet, but a fast, which is accompanied by prayer. It's a time when you get off the throne of your heart and Jesus becomes your master. He will do a supernatural work in your life if you'll fast and pray.

4. Keep yourselves accountable to someone.

A director of an alcoholic treatment center asks two questions when people are readmitted for treatment:

"When did you stop going to support meetings?"

"What are you hiding?"[3]

Both are valid questions. Accountability and honesty prevent stumbling.

Find a support group or an accountability partner. "Iron sharpens iron, so one man sharpens another" (Prov. 27:17). Your accountability partner needs to be "iron"—tough enough to ask the hard questions and strong enough to sharpen you.

A little boy went to a store to buy a birthday present for his mother. He asked the salesclerk if he could see their cookie jars. The clerk showed him a counter with several different-shaped containers on display. The youngster carefully lifted and replaced each lid, then asked, "Do you have any jars that don't have noisy lids?"

People do things in secret because they don't want anyone to know. You can safeguard yourself against secret sins by admitting your weaknesses to a Christian friend. Let that person hold you accountable for your actions. Meeting with another believer once or twice a week to pray through your struggles will help prevent temptation.

Accountability establishes a safeguard to keep you from slipping into a secret world. If you don't make yourself accountable, you might privately keep raiding the cookie jar.

Confide in a trusted Christian friend of your gender, who will hold you accountable for your actions. If you struggle with homosexuality, it might be best to entrust yourself to a Christian of the opposite sex. Give him or her an honest report of your area of weakness. Christian fellowship is essential in maintaining your freedom.

Take one day at a time. God never intended us to live a month at a time. With Christ's help, anyone can live successfully for twenty-four hours. Make it through today and then live through tomorrow in the same way.

Victory is won—one day at a time.

THIRTEEN

Worry Glasses:
The Movies in Your Mind

*I've suffered a great many catastrophes in my life. Most of
them never happened.*

~ MARK TWAIN

M ARCH 1994. Three men, copying a movie they had just
seen, shot and killed a retail clerk and then robbed a
store. Within hours the group struck again, robbing a florist
and a pizzeria. Detective Doug Hummel of the Oakland
County, California, Sheriff's Department explained, "All of
them had apparently watched the film (*Menace II Society*) several times and were acting out parts of it."[1]

March 1995. Fifteen-year-old Jason Lewis carried his
father's shotgun into the living room of his family's mobile
home, where he brutally murdered his unsuspecting parents.
He had just seen the movie *Natural Born Killers* and was acting out what he had seen on the screen.[2]

June 1998. A woman on a cruise ship off Sweden climbed out on the bow and spread her arms, imitating Rose's famous scene in the movie *Titanic*. Her next action, however, did not go according to script. She lost her footing, then fell into the ocean and drowned. Nearly two dozen copycat incidences of people reenacting this movie scene on ships' bows caused the Passenger Vessel Association to issue a "Titanic alert" to its cruise operators.[3]

When was the last time you watched a movie? I don't mean in that cinema at the mall. I'm talking about the movies in your mind. Satan has produced a wide variety of films that he wants you to view.

A seat has been reserved for you. The popcorn is ready. The lights have been turned down, and the show is about to begin. Admission is free. All Satan requires is that you believe what you see.

He projects his films onto the movie screen of your mind, trying to convince you that what you see is real. Although the movies in your mind are imaginary, *worry glasses* make every scene appear in 3-D as though it were actually happening. The devil wants you to react to what you see, just as the people acted out what they saw in the movie theaters. By making deception appear as reality, he can manipulate your behavior.

∿ Acting on Belief

Several years ago someone called a package delivery driver's wife in Kansas while her husband was on the road. A man in a professional-sounding voice said, "Mrs. Jones, this is Dr. Johnson. I'm sorry to inform you that your husband is in the hospital with a life-threatening, unknown disease and may die. We need a hair sample from you immediately because we believe you may have also contracted this disease."

The terrible news jolted the poor woman. The man instructed her to get a pair of scissors and cut off all her hair at the roots so the hospital could run some lab tests. She obediently did as she was ordered, cutting off her hair.

> Satan wants our *perception* to be based upon *deception.*

After completing the caller's instructions, she asked what to do next.

The man replied, "The next thing you need to do is wait for your husband to come home. I made up this entire story." The prankster then hung up.

Satan wants our *perception* to be based upon *deception.* This woman acted on what she believed to be true. We act, not necessarily upon what is true but on what we *believe* to be true. Satan also knows this, so he creates an unreal world through our imaginations. He knows that if he can get us to believe his lies, we'll react as though they were true.

That's why he projects his disaster movies onto the screens of our minds. As we watch these imaginary horror flicks, we experience agony and despair as we view every catastrophe imaginable. We see plane crashes . . . car wrecks . . . incurable diseases . . . and financial crises. Although none of the events have occurred, we writhe in anguish as we watch each terrifying scene. Our frantic imaginations manipulate our emotions like a puppet on a string.

A lady had pain in her hand, so she looked up "arthritis" in her medical book. After reading a couple of pages, she knew she had arthritis in every joint in her body. She read a few pages about ulcers. "Now I know what's causing the pain in my stomach," she muttered. As she continued to read, she realized she had nearly every disease in the book. She made an appointment to see the doctor. After doing an examination, the doctor scribbled a prescription and handed it to her. The lady opened the note and read, "Stop reading medical books."

When we nurture fearful thoughts, we can convince ourselves that the imaginations are real. Deception fights against reality for control of our minds. Imaginations are Satan's decoys to trick us into fighting the wrong battles.

During World War II, Americans made hundreds of inflatable tanks and airplanes, the same size and shape as armored tanks and aircraft. Although the decoys would not fool anyone if seen up close, they looked authentic when viewed from a distance. The U.S. Army used the phony tanks to trick the Nazis into believing American troops were entrenched in a certain location. The plan worked. The German forces attacked the dummy tanks and planes instead of the real ones.

When we watch Satan's horror movies, we exhaust ourselves fighting decoys. And we fail to notice the demon laughing behind the movie projector.

Take Off Your Glasses

Want to quit worrying? Here are three ways to conquer your fearful outlook on life.

1. Pray instead of worry.

A husband asked his wife why she was always worrying. "You know it doesn't do any good," he said.

"Oh yes, it does," she replied. "Over 90 percent of the things I worry about never happen."

Most of the things we worry about will never occur. The other concerns either won't be as bad as we think, or God will give us the grace to endure them.

The Lord gave us the weapon of prayer to combat worry. God designed prayer to be a courier service to deliver our problems into His hands. "Don't worry about anything; instead, pray about everything. Tell God what you need, and thank him for all he has done." (Phil. 4:6, NLT). If we still worry after we've finished praying, we never actually prayed in the first place. It was just a religious ritual.

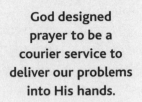

God designed prayer to be a courier service to deliver our problems into His hands.

Prayer *worriers* don't trust because they worry. They don't believe God can help them in their time of need. Although they may mumble prayers with their lips, they never trust God to take care of their problems.

Prayer *warriors* don't worry because they trust. They come boldly before the throne of grace to find help in time of need. Their faith in God overrules their worry.

Are you a worrier or a warrior?

Worrying can be more stressful on us than actually going through what we fear. My son Scott transferred from a small private school to a large middle school in seventh grade. He had to make numerous adjustments and hated every one of them. He constantly complained about having to attend the new school.

I prayed with him every night and gave him some fatherly advice. "Scott, don't worry about it. It's not as bad as you think."

He responded, "Dad, it's not that easy. It's hard not to worry."

By November I noticed he hadn't said anything about disliking the new school. "Scott," I asked, "You seem more relaxed than you were a month ago. Are you still having problems adjusting to school?"

He answered, "Yes, but I quit worrying about it. I found out that worrying was harder on me than actually going through it."

Many people never learn that it's usually more draining to worry than it is to experience the thing they dread. Prayer can remove the weight of worry.

2. Cast down fearful imaginations.

If a horror movie begins to roll on the screen of your mind, take immediate action by "casting down" the imagination. Paul wrote about the importance of "casting down imaginations, and every high thing that exalteth itself against the knowledge of God" (2 Cor. 10:5, KJV).

Stop this imaginative film by commanding the thoughts to leave in Jesus' name. The Lord has given His children authority over all of Satan's power. "Behold, I have given you authority to tread on serpents and scorpions, and over all the power of the enemy, and nothing will injure you. Nevertheless do not rejoice in this, that the spirits are subject to you, but rejoice that your names are recorded in heaven" (Luke 10:19, 20).

Taking authority over demonic imaginations is crucial in making those thoughts leave. If you don't forcefully take a stand, the movies in your mind will continue to torment you. "Submit therefore to God. Resist the devil and he will flee from you" (James 4:7). Satan must leave when you take a stand to oppose him. If you will resist the devil, he will vacate the premises and take his movie projector with him.

3. Saturate your mind with God's thoughts.

Second Corinthians 10:5 continues, "[Bring] into captivity every thought to the obedience of Christ" (KJV). After we cast down the imagination, godly thoughts won't automatically rush into our minds. We must go after and capture them.

Uprooting weeds isn't enough. We have to plant grass in the soil where the weeds used to live. If we don't replant the barren area, it won't be long before the weeds grow back.

Casting down imaginations without taking every thought captive invites worry to return. If we occupy our minds with uplifting thoughts, the weeds won't have any room to grow. We can occupy our minds by purposely and continually thinking godly thoughts.

In the middle of a wedding ceremony, a jewelry store manager exchanged rings with his soon-to-be spouse. As he slipped the ring onto his bride's finger, he said, "With this ring—we guarantee a full refund if the customer is not completely satisfied."

His sales pitch was so deeply ingrained in his mind that the words came out automatically.

What's ingrained in your mind? You can saturate your mind with godly thoughts by meditating on Scriptures, reading Christian literature, praying, and praising. "Whatever is true, whatever is honorable, whatever is right, whatever is pure, whatever is lovely, whatever is of good repute, if there is any excellence and if anything worthy of praise, dwell on these things" (Phil. 4:8).

4. Trust God.

Worry never trusts. Trust never worries.

Make a conscious decision to go against your own speculations and trust God's Word. "Trust in the Lord with all your heart and do not lean on your own understanding" (Prov. 3:5).

Scuba divers can get disoriented when they're deep underwater because of the way light is diffused through water. They feel weightless, which makes it easy to lose their sense of direction. When divers don't know which way is up, they remember their training, which has taught them to disregard their own sense of direction and follow their air bubbles. If the air bubbles appear to be going sideways, the diver must override his own logic and trust the bubbles. Air bubbles always go up—they're right every time.

Worry tells you the worst is going to happen. This confuses your spiritual guidance system, which makes you panic. Many people are misled by worry because they abandon the Lord's guidance during times of crisis.

God's Word will direct your steps, just as air bubbles guide scuba divers. To follow the Lord's leading you must disregard your own sense of direction. Trusting in the Lord will displace worry, destroy imaginations, and calm your fears.

Take off your glasses. Sure is nice not being tormented, isn't it?

Discouragement Glasses: At the End of Your Rope

Life is full of obstacle illusions.

~ GRANT FRAZIER

DO YOU LIVE where never is heard an encouraging word, and the skies are cloudy all day? And no one appreciates you, right?

I hear you. I've thought about checking out of my own responsibilities a few hundred times myself. Throughout the years I've watched dozens of people quit. They go into a tailspin and never seem to recover. That's not the answer.

It's easy to slip on the *discouragement glasses* when everything goes wrong. When we look through these dark spectacles, we lose hope for tomorrow. We're ready to resign from the human race, thinking there's no reason to continue.

A tree is best measured when it's down. That's true with people too. Being down doesn't mean being done. Sometimes we must get to the end of our ropes to experience God in a new way.

During the 1930s, 250 men were holding the ropes to a dirigible (an airship similar to a blimp) to keep it from floating away. Suddenly a gust of wind caught one end of the dirigible, lifting it high off the ground. Some of the men immediately

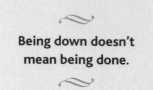

Being down doesn't mean being done.

let go of their ropes and fell safely to the ground. Others panicked, clinging firmly to the end of their ropes as the nose of the dirigible arose to greater heights. Several men who couldn't keep holding on fell and were seriously injured. One man, however, continued to dangle high in the air for forty-five minutes until he was rescued. Reporters later asked him how he was able to hold on to the rope for so long. "I didn't hold on to the rope," he replied. "I just tied it around my waist, and the rope held on to me."

David was once at the end of his rope and learned to let God hold him up. You do remember David, don't you? The sheep-tending, rock-slinging, giant-killing, wife-stealing, song-writing guy who penned the Twenty-third Psalm? He didn't spend *all* his time lying in green pastures beside still waters. Sometimes he had to walk through death valley and sit at a table in the presence of his enemies.

One day when David and his men returned to the city of Ziklag, they discovered that the Amalekites had burned the city down and had taken their wives and children captive. David fell to his knees, along with the six hundred men with him, and they wept until their strength was gone (see 1 Sam. 30:3–6).

Just when he thought things couldn't get any worse, David overheard the men whispering behind his back, "If we hadn't left our families to follow David, none of this would have happened. This is David's fault. Let's stone him and make him pay for the loss of our families."

Murphy's Law, not to be confused with Moses' Law, was in effect that day. David was fleeing from Saul. His family had been kidnapped. His own men were threatening to kill him. His house had been burned down. And he probably forgot to renew his fire insurance policy.

David was at the lowest point of his life. Discouragement had sapped all the strength out of his heart. He had reached the end of his rope. It would have been easy for him to give up.

When Lord Horatio Nelson was fighting the Battle of Copenhagen, his senior officer, Sir Hyde Parker, also known as "Old Vinegar," hoisted the flag signaling retreat. Nelson deliberately put his telescope to his blind eye and said, "I do not see it."

If he had surrendered when it looked like defeat, he would not have captured twelve Danish ships.

I don't see defeat. Do you?

When you're fighting the Battle of Perspective, Satan will hoist his flag, trying to discourage you. Remember to put a blind eye to the telescope. Refuse to see the retreat flag. Keep going forward.

David knew he couldn't keep going forward on his own energy. He had no friends to whisper encouraging words. His only hope was for God to have mercy on him.

Charles Spurgeon said, "Sometimes God sends His mercies in a black envelope." David opened the black envelope and read this message: "Once God has spoken; Twice I have heard this: That power belongs to God" (Ps. 62:11). He called out to a power higher than himself to strengthen him. Like the apostle Paul, he discovered that God's power is perfected in weakness (see 2 Cor. 12:9).

Maybe discouragement has drained the last ounce of energy out of your heart. You're at the end of your rope. Your fingers are slipping. Does the end of your rope mean the end of your hope? Nope.

The end of your rope is the beginning of hope! It's the place where you stop trusting in you and start trusting in God. Only after you have exhausted your own strength will you discover that God's mercy and grace are sufficient for you.

> ~
> **The end of your rope is the beginning of hope.**
> ~

~ Take Off Your Glasses

The following anonymous poem gives wise counsel to those who are going through a difficult time:

When things go wrong, as they sometimes will.
When the road you're trudging seems all uphill,
When funds are low and debts are high
And you want to smile, but you have to sigh,
When care is pressing you down a bit—
Rest if you must, but don't you quit.

Life is strange with its twists and turns,
As everyone of us sometimes learns;
And many a failure turns about,
When he might have won had he stuck it out.
Don't give up, though the pace seems slow;
You may succeed with another blow.

Often the goal is nearer than
It seems to a faint and faltering man;
Often the struggler has given up
When he might have captured the victor's cup;
And he learned too late, when the night slipped down,
How close he was to the golden crown.

Success is failure turned inside out
The silver tint in the clouds of doubt;
And you cannot tell how close you are,
It may be near when it seems afar.
So stick to the fight when you're hardest hit;
It's when things seem worst that you mustn't quit.[1]

1. Look for the reward beyond the obstacle.

Henry Ford said, "Obstacles are those frightful things you see when you take your eyes off your goal." Don't let the obstruction in your path keep you from reaching your destination.

A king placed a huge boulder on a roadway. He hid and watched to see if anyone would remove the roadblock. Some saw the huge rock in the road and walked around it. Others blamed the king for not keeping the roads clear. No one made an attempt to move the boulder.

A little while later a peasant came along. He realized the obstruction presented a problem for everyone traveling on that road, so he decided to remove it. He pushed on the rock with all his might, but it wouldn't budge. As he continued to press against the boulder, it slowly began to roll. Finally he was able to move the obstacle off the road.

When he turned around, he noticed a bag lying where the boulder had been. Inside the purse he discovered gold coins and a note from the king. It read, "This reward goes to the one who moved the boulder off the path."

Obstacles are put in the way to see if we really want something or just thought we did.

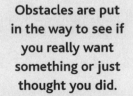

Obstacles are put in the way to see if you really want something or just thought you did.

Sometimes the reward isn't always apparent. A boulder is covering it up. We won't receive the prize until we've removed the obstruction and finished the task.

No difficulty you encounter is greater than the grace of God. "He gives a greater grace" (James 4:6). His grace is more powerful than any problem you will face.

2. Stay confident in the midst of uncertainty.

We must keep our composure during difficult times because confidence promises a great reward. "Do not throw away your confidence, which has a great reward. For you have need of endurance, so that when you have done the will of God, you may receive what was promised" (Heb. 10:35, 36). The demon of discouragement wants us to throw away our confidence so we will forfeit the reward.

I've never met a confident discouraged person. If we took a vote of confidence, the nays would have it. It's hard to endure trying times without being empowered by the Holy Spirit.

Several children in a park watched a man release helium-filled balloons. The man let go of a white balloon, which floated up into the sky. Then he released yellow and red balloons, which also flew up and away. A little African-American boy asked, "Mister, if you let go of a black balloon, will it go up?"

The man replied, "Son, the color on the outside has nothing to do with it. It's what's on the inside that makes it go up."

When God's uplifting Spirit fills your heart, you'll confidently rise above the clouds of discouragement.

3. Keep knocking on closed doors.

Many of God's blessings are waiting behind doors that are yet to be knocked on. God wants us to be persistent. Keep asking. Keep seeking. Keep knocking. Jesus said, "Ask, and it shall be given to you; seek, and you will find; knock, and it will be opened to you" (Matt. 7:7).

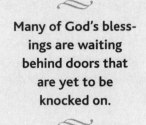

Many of God's blessings are waiting behind doors that are yet to be knocked on.

We'll never know which door has the treasure on the other side until we knock on the right one. It could be door number ninety-nine. The demon of discouragement tries to convince us that the door will never open and we might as well quit knocking on it.

Late one afternoon when the office was about to close, a business manager finally allowed a life insurance salesman to see him. The manager told the salesman, "You should feel highly honored. Do you know that I have refused to see seven insurance men today?"

"I know," replied the agent. "I'm them."[2]

God loves to bless His children who keep knocking after everyone else has clocked out and gone home. Because most people are looking for shortcuts, persistence is the most overlooked means of receiving God's blessings. It's the long, hard way to receive good things from God, and most people aren't willing to take that route.

Scientists have proven the power of persistence through an experiment using an iron ball and a cork. A one-ton iron ball was suspended from the ceiling using a metal cable. A small cork hung by a thread next to the heavy ball. An electrical mechanism kept the cork gently bouncing against the iron weight.

After many days of constant pounding by the cork, the researchers noticed the iron ball starting to move ever so slightly. The cork continued to knock against it until the heavy ball swung widely back and forth on its own.

Although we might think that we aren't making progress, the door will open if we will keep knocking. Our persistent faith will be the difference in moving the mountains in our lives.

> Persistence is the most overlooked means of receiving God's blessing.

4. Remember that God has the last word.

God may not have spoken the first word in the difficulty you're experiencing, but He does have the last word. The Lord is still on His throne—no matter how gloomy things may appear. You can still have hope, even when things don't go the way you think they should.

I don't understand why some things happen the way they do, but I do know that God causes all things to work together for good to those who love Him (Rom. 8:28). Knowing that God is in ultimate control gives me encouragement to keep going when times get rough.

It kept David going, too. After he strengthened himself in the Lord, he rallied the troops together, conquered the Amalekites, and recovered everything they had taken. That would not have been possible if he hadn't first removed his discouragement glasses.

Take off your glasses and look outside. The sun is shining, the antelope are playing, and I don't hear any more discouraging words. Are you feeling better?

I hope you now understand that the end of your rope doesn't mean the end of your hope. It's the beginning of a new adventure with God.

PART 3

Correcting Your Perspective

F OR CENTURIES, people believed the sun revolved around the earth. They had proof—the sun rose in the east and set in the west. And it looked so small compared to our planet. Scientists balked when Nicolaus Copernicus suggested the earth revolved around the sun. It never occurred to them that they might be seeing with the wrong perspective.

Truth prevailed. People corrected their perspectives to line up with the facts.

Some people today actually believe the world revolves *around them.* They see themselves as the center of the universe and bristle when God's Word suggests otherwise.

How do you know when you're seeing with the right perspective?

You'll know when your life revolves around the Son.

FIFTEEN

Seeing as God Sees

The real voyage of discovery consists of not in seeking new landscapes but in having new eyes.

~MARCEL PROUST

YOU ARE sitting in your living room watching a football game on television. The referee throws a penalty flag against your team. You yell, "Hey, ref! Are you blind? That wasn't a penalty!" You know he made an incorrect call because you watched the play from your point of view.

Then the camera shows a replay from a different angle. When you view the play from another vantage point, you discover that the referee actually did make the correct call. You were mistaken because you couldn't see the entire picture from your limited perspective.

To get the right perspective in life, we need to view our circumstances from heaven's point of view. If we look at our situation from God's perspective, we'll interpret what happens to us in a different light. "The Lord looks from heaven; He sees all the sons of men; From His dwelling place He looks out on all the inhabitants of the earth" (Ps. 33:13, 14).

The Lord *looks* from heaven. God has perfect vision from His heavenly throne. The secret of a happy, fulfilling life is to view our existence through God's eyes.

When a person receives an eye transplant, the patient sees through someone else's eyes. The Lord wants to give us His eyes so we can see as He sees.

Here are four things we must see to have 20/20 spiritual vision:

1. See God in control.

Think how our perspective would change if we viewed every circumstance as God views it. We would look beyond the earthly realm and see Him in control. Faith is the ability to look past adverse circumstances and see God's hand at work.

Jesus had this perspective during His earthly life. He said, "Truly, truly, I say to you, the Son can do nothing of Himself, unless it is something He sees the Father doing" (John 5:19). Christ always saw His Father's hand at work. He knew His Father was in control, even when He stood on trial before Pontius Pilate. "Pilate said to Him . . . 'Do You not know that I have authority to release You, and I have authority to crucify You?' Jesus answered, 'You would have no authority over Me, unless it had been given you from above'" (John 19:10, 11).

From an earthly standpoint, it appeared as though Pilate was in charge. Christ, however, informed him that he had been granted power by a higher authority. He knew that Pilate couldn't do anything without the Father's approval.

Why would Christ appoint Judas Iscariot, the one who would betray him, to be His treasurer? Judas had a bad habit of stealing some of the offerings out of the money box (John 12:6).

Only a fool—or someone who completely trusted in God's sovereignty—would put a traitor in that position.

We don't see Jesus saying: "Father, I can't believe You had me choose Judas to be My disciple and treasurer! What were You thinking?"

Jesus always saw His Father in control and rested in that fact. We also need to see the Father's hand at work in our lives, even when things aren't going our way. We must view life from a higher perspective. We must submit ourselves to His lordship, and look for His hand to intervene in our situations.

Joseph viewed life from this higher perspective. When his brothers sold him into slavery, he didn't put on rejection glasses. When he was falsely accused by Potiphar's wife and unjustly thrown into prison, he refused to wear bitterness glasses. Instead, he trusted God when circumstances didn't make sense.

Years later God promoted him to being a ruler in Egypt. When Joseph was reunited with his brothers, he told them that he viewed their actions from God's perspective:

> Do not be grieved or angry with yourselves, because you sold me here, for God sent me before you to preserve life. . . . God sent me before you to preserve for you a remnant in the earth, and to keep you alive by a great deliverance. . . . It was not you who sent me here, but God (Gen. 45:5, 7, 8).

Trusting in the Lord's sovereignty simply means we believe God has the final word in all that happens. "The Lord has established His throne in the heavens, and His sovereignty rules over all" (Ps. 103:19).

Some people misunderstand God's sovereignty. They think it means that God causes all kinds of tragedies just to make people angry with Him. As Paul wrote, "This persuasion did not come from Him who calls you" (Gal. 5:8). God is for you, not against you (Rom. 8:31).

Trust fills the gap when we don't understand.

God's sovereignty means that He can overrule what others intend for evil and bring about a good result. Joseph told his brothers, "You meant evil against me, but God meant it for good in order to bring about this present result, to preserve many people alive" (Gen. 50:20).

The Lord doesn't always let us in on what He's doing. Trust fills the gap when we don't understand. We must give the Father the benefit of the doubt—that He will work all things together for good to those who love Him (Rom. 8:28).

2. View life from a victor's perspective.

When Arnold Palmer was playing in the West Penn junior finals as a high school student, he missed a short putt. He became so upset that he threw his putter over the gallery into a clump of trees. Arnold quickly forgot about the missed putt when he was awarded a trophy for winning the tournament. On the way home his father told him, "If you ever throw a club again, you'll never play in another golf tournament."[1]

His father was disappointed in the way his son reacted when things didn't go his way. If Arnold had known he was going to win the tournament, he wouldn't have tossed the golf club because the putt didn't change the outcome.

Have you thrown any putters lately? If so, it might be because you can't see yourself winning. If you're a Christian, God has already determined that you will be victorious.

Who will separate us from the love of Christ? Shall tribula-
tion, or distress, or persecution, or famine, or nakedness, or
peril, or sword? Just as it is written, "For Your sake we are
being put to death all day long; We were considered as sheep
to be slaughtered." But in all these things we overwhelmingly
conquer through Him who loved us (Rom. 8:35–37).

The Lord has already announced that His children overwhelmingly conquer. You are on the winning side! Do you
view your life from the standpoint of victory?

At the height of World War II, the British army was
entrenched in North Africa to defend the Suez Canal from the
Nazis. Field Marshal Erwin Rommel, Germany's notorious
"Desert Fox," started moving his troops across Libya. His
forces rolled victoriously into Egypt.

British troops were demoralized because their armored tank
force was decimated. They had retreated hundreds of miles and
their backs were to the Suez, facing a seemingly invincible foe.

In August 1942 General Bernard Montgomery took field
command to the battered British 8th Army in Egypt.
Montgomery was an optimistic man and a brilliant field tac-
tician. One day he and a subordinate climbed up on a desert
dune to scout Rommel's camp. Montgomery said, "It's a sad
thing that a professional soldier should reach the peak of his
generalship and then suffer defeat."

The subordinate was alarmed that the usually optimistic
general would sound so hopeless. "Don't be discouraged, sir.
We may still win."

The general replied, "Of course we will win. I wasn't talking about my defeat. I'm talking about Rommel!"

Montgomery routed Rommel's forces and drove the
Germans eastward, clear across North Africa. The Desert Fox
from Germany never won another battle in the African desert.[2]

By faith you can foresee the outcome of your earthly struggles. God has already declared victory. Now you just need to view life as a winner. Do you see it?

3. Look at people as valuable.

Years ago the prime minister of France summoned a prominent doctor to perform surgery on him. The statesman told him, "I expect to be treated like royalty and not like the common person in the hospital."

"Don't worry," the surgeon replied. "All my patients are prime ministers in my eyes."

We need to view everyone as a prime minister. Most people don't see others like that. They look through *prejudiced glasses* and view some people as less valuable than others. They don't realize that everyone has equal value in God's eyes. "The rich and the poor have a common bond. The Lord is the maker of them all" (Prov. 22:2). The homeless man lying in the gutter is just as precious as the most admired movie star. Only by looking through God's eyes will we see everyone as priceless.

Jesus saw everyone through the eyes of love. "*Seeing* the people, He *felt compassion* for them, because they were distressed and dispirited like sheep without a shepherd" (Matt. 9:36, author's emphasis). He saw them with compassion because He created each individual and would die for each one as well.

Do you view others in this way? Every person, even the obnoxious one, is a person Christ spilled His blood for. That makes everyone valuable in His eyes.

A well-known speaker began his seminar by holding up a twenty dollar bill. He asked everyone at the conference, "Who would like this new twenty dollar bill?" Hands went up all over the room.

SEEING AS GOD SEES

He said, "I'm going to give this twenty dollar bill to one of you, but first I need to crumple it." He wadded up the bill and asked, "Who still wants it?"

Hands were quickly raised. The speaker dropped the bill and ground it into the floor with his shoe. He picked up the crumpled, dirty bill.

"Now who wants it?" Everyone still lifted their hands.

"Friends, you've all learned a valuable lesson," the speaker concluded. "No matter what I did to the money, you still want it because its value hasn't changed. Even though the bill is crumpled and dirty, it's still worth twenty dollars." Although someone may have been misused and abused, he or she still has infinite worth. Every person is precious in His sight.

Do you see others—and yourself—as priceless?

4. View every day with an eternal perspective.

A doctor told his patient, "I have good news and bad news. The good news is that you have only one week to live."

"That's the *good* news? What's the bad news?"

"The bad news is that I was supposed to tell you last week, but I forgot."

If you found out that you had only a week to live, how would you view life? You need to view every day as if it were your last. You don't know when your life will end.

The length of our earthly life is merely a moment when compared to eternity. "You are just a vapor that appears for a little while and then vanishes away" (James 4:14). Visit a cemetery and read the dates engraved on the headstones. The deceased's days on earth were numbered and are now over. What did that person live for?

One day our names will be chiseled on headstones. How are we spending our allotted days on earth? We must keep an eternal perspective every day, mindful that we're quickly passing through this world. Life on earth is simply a dressing room for eternity. An eternal world awaits us after death.

> One day your name will be chiseled on a headstone.

We need to make every day count because our time on earth is running out. "Teach us to number our days, that we may present to You a heart of wisdom" (Ps. 90:12). Numbering our days means we're continually aware that life could end at any moment, and we want each day to have an eternal purpose.

A man started thinking about how much time he had left to live and how he could measure it. He calculated that the average person lives seventy-five years, which would include 3,900 Saturdays. Since he was fifty-five years old, he had already lived through nearly 2,900 Saturdays. If he lived twenty more years, he would have about a thousand Saturdays left.

He went to several toy stores and bought a thousand marbles, which he put inside a clear container. Every Saturday he took one marble out of the jar and threw it away. By watching the marbles decrease in the jar, he was reminded that time was running out and that he needed to focus on important things in life. Measuring how much time he had left helped him keep an eternal perspective.

When he turned seventy-five, he took the last marble out of the container and said, "I figure that if I make it until next Saturday, God has given me a little extra time on earth."

That man viewed his life in light of eternity. You can make every day count for eternity by living to please the Lord in all that you do.

Let me suggest a few eye-opening exercises to keep your perspective fresh:

⌇ Exercising Your Perspective

- *Look down out of an airplane.*
  A friend told me his perspective changes when he looks
  out an airplane window as it rises in the air after take-
  off. It makes him realize how little he is when viewed
  from a higher perspective.
- *Take a mission trip to a third-world country.*
  See how most of the world lives and it will open your
  eyes to how much you have.
- *Drive through a poverty-stricken neighborhood.*
  Picture yourself growing up in one of those houses.
  Think what it's like to view life from a poverty-level
  income.
- *Minister to elderly people in rest homes.*
  Take the time to talk with those who are at the end of
  their lives. What did they regret? Are they ready to face
  death? If they aren't ready to face God, talk to them
  about their relationship with the Lord. Teach a Bible
  study, sing, or pray with them.
- *Sit in a hospital emergency waiting room.*
  Comfort those people, and pray with the friends and
  family of loved ones.
- *Take sandwiches to homeless people or volunteer at a res-
  cue shelter.*
  Think what it would be like to change places with them.
  Imagine what it would be like to have no hope to ever
  have a good job or live in a nice house.
- *Walk through a cemetery.*
  Some of my most special moments are when I walk
  through cemeteries and read the headstones. It makes
  me realize that my body will be in that dirt one day.
  Think about the shortness of life, the length of eternity,
  and the meaning of life.

- *Read the obituary column.*
  One day your picture will be in the column. What will be said about how you lived?

In the next chapter I'll show you another revolutionary exercise that will help you see as God sees.

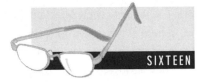

SIXTEEN

Focusing on Blessings

It is only with the heart that one can see rightly.

~ ANTOINE DE SAINT-EXUPERY

ONE AFTERNOON my wife, Cindy, called me from the bank where she worked. "The diamond fell out of my wedding ring!" she sobbed. "It broke loose from the ring prongs, and I don't know where it is!"

My mind flashed back two decades, while as a poor seminary student surviving on peanut butter and jelly sandwiches and cheap buffets, I saved $750 to purchase the most beautiful diamond ring in the world for my future wife. Diamond appraisers wouldn't describe it that way, of course. Less than half a karat. Small carbon flaw. However, the true worth of a diamond isn't determined by karats and clarity but by the love with which it's purchased.

This diamond had collected numerous memories as a traveling companion through our nineteen years of marriage. It was a tenant in our first apartment and visited the hospital when our children were born. It was a frequent passenger in our $300 car, which left a trail of black smoke signals wherever we drove. That jewel had been a silent witness as it journeyed with us through good times and bad.

The chances of finding it were slim to none. We had no earthly idea where it could be hiding. Cindy could have lost it in our house while getting ready for work, at the restaurant where she had gone for lunch, or somewhere in the bank.

Lord, I prayed, *You know where Cindy lost her diamond. Please show me where it is.*

Immediately I felt prompted to go to the bank parking lot to begin my search. When I arrived, the first place I looked was inside my wife's minivan. Nothing in there. When I turned around to scan the lot, I saw something glisten. Tiny rocks and small chunks of gravel covered the parking lot. As I drew closer to investigate, my heart leaped when I discovered Cindy's diamond lying in a crack in the pavement. I snatched up the diamond and ran into the bank lobby holding it high for everyone to see.

"Look—I found it!" I yelled.

Bank customers turned around to find out why I was causing such a commotion. Cindy looked up from behind her teller window, burst into tears, and came running through the lobby into my arms. As we hugged in the middle of the bank in front of the customers, we looked like the final scene of a romantic movie.

Although we hadn't noticed the diamond that morning, it became the center of our attention that evening. We called our friends and relatives to tell them how our lost diamond had been found and then went out to dinner to celebrate.

Our lost diamond incident bore an uncanny resemblance to the parable of the lost coin (see Luke 15:8, 9). The woman in the parable lost a silver coin, searched diligently, and found it. She was so excited that she called all her friends and neighbors to share her joy. After finding our lost jewel, Cindy and I had unwittingly followed the same script as the woman in the parable.

> The value of something isn't determined by how much it appreciates, but by how much it is appreciated.

Had the value of the diamond changed? No.

What had changed? Our perception of its value.

I learned one of the great secrets of thankfulness through this adventure. The value of something isn't determined by how much it appreciates, but by how much it is appreciated.

Maybe everybody needs to lose a diamond. That way the whole world could rediscover the gift of appreciation.

～ Blinded to Blessings

Imagine for a moment that you live in a beautiful mansion with a scenic view of the countryside. You own the finest furniture. Paintings by Monet hang in your hallway. Your yard is landscaped with exotic flowers and cascading waterfalls. Your dining room displays the finest china, and a Rolls Royce occupies your garage.

Add one more factor to your hypothetical world. You're blind. Although you possess all these material blessings, you can't see any of them. Your blindness greatly diminishes your ability to appreciate the things you own.

Cursed is the person who is surrounded by blessings but is unable to see them.

Bill Gates, the founder and chief executive officer of Microsoft, was the speaker at a convention in Seattle. Gates is one of the richest men in the United States, with personal wealth of $35 billion. At the end of his speech, he allowed the audience to ask questions. One man asked, "Mr. Gates, if you were blind, would you trade all your money to have your sight restored?"

Bill Gates replied that he would indeed exchange all his money to regain eyesight. He put a $35 billion price tag on his ability to see.

> Cursed is the person who is surrounded by blessings, but is unable to see them.

What price tag have you placed on your vision? Although you may have eyesight, you might not be able to see your blessings. It's easy to take good things for granted. The danger of familiarity is that you stop appreciating what you have.

Moses gave this warning:

> When you have eaten and are satisfied, you shall bless the Lord your God for the good land which He has given you. Beware that you do not forget the Lord your God. . . . Otherwise, when you have eaten and are satisfied, and have built good houses and lived in them, and when your herds and your flocks multiply, and your silver and gold multiply, and all that you have multiplies, then your heart will become proud and you will forget the Lord your God who brought you out from the land of Egypt, out of the house of slavery" (Deut. 8:10, 14).

A friend of mine lives on the coast of Florida a few miles from Kennedy Space Center. I told him, "It must be fun watching the space shuttle launches and going to the beach all the time."

"I never go to the beach," he replied. "I don't even go outside my house to watch the space shuttle launch."

"You're kidding me. Why?" I asked.

"I've seen them so many times it's no big deal."

When we see the same blessings every day, we eventually stop noticing them.

When we stop noticing, we quit appreciating.

When we quit appreciating, we stop thanking.

When we stop thanking, we start complaining.

At this point, we have forgotten the Lord our God, who provided all the things we enjoy (see 1 Tim. 6:17). We won't forget the Lord if we continually give thanks. How can we cultivate this attitude? By using reference points.

◌ Reference Points

A man lived in a tiny hut with his wife, two small children, and his elderly parents. He tried to be patient with the crowded conditions, but the noise and congestion was more than he could take. In desperation, he consulted the village wise man.

The wise man asked, "Do you have a rooster?"

"Yes," he replied.

"Move your rooster into your hut, and come see me again next week." The man didn't understand, but the wise man had never given bad advice before.

The next week, he returned and told the wise man that his living conditions had grown worse. The rooster was always crowing and making a mess in the hut.

The wise man asked, "Do you have a cow?"

The man nodded reluctantly.

"Move your cow into your hut, and come see me next week."

Over the next several weeks, on the advice of the wise elder, the man also made room for a goat, two dogs, and his brother's children.

The man couldn't take it any longer. He went to the wise man in a fit of rage. "My situation is worse than ever. What do you expect me to do now?"

The wise man replied, "Go home and remove all the guests from your hut."

He hurried home and kicked out all the animals and relatives, leaving only his wife, children, and parents. Suddenly his perspective changed, and he was overjoyed to have such a spacious, quiet house.[1]

> Reference points give you a mental price tag to help you see the value of your blessings.

The wise man made him create a reference point for thankfulness. A reference point is a predicament that's worse than what we're currently experiencing. Any situation can look good if compared with a worse set of circumstances.

Reference points give us a mental price tag to help us see the value of our blessings. How much is a glass of water worth? It depends whether we're in a desert or a swimming pool. The value of an item is determined by how badly it's wanted.

Here are five common reference points that will increase your ability to appreciate.

Reference point #1: Theoretically trading places

Over 90 percent of the world's population would be thrilled to change places with you right now, no questions asked. Robert Orben says, "The next time you feel like complaining, just remember that your garbage disposal eats better than 30 percent of the world."

The starving people in India would love to trade places with you. They could sit at your dining room table filled with delicious food, and you could sit on the rat infested streets of Calcutta. How would you like that? Would you prefer to exchange living conditions with someone in the bitter cold of

Siberia? How about someone in the poverty stricken villages of Mexico?

Complaining about your car? Swap places with the millions of people around the world who would love to have your clunker right now, and you can ride a burrow to your next destination. Multitudes would love to have your clean water. Exchange your bottle of purified water for their water filled with parasites. Remember, God has His eye on the people in India, Siberia, and Mexico at the same time He's watching you.

You can become thankful by acknowledging how much you have compared to most of the rest of the world. God didn't bless you so that you would feel guilty for having good things. He just wants you to be grateful to Him and to help the less fortunate. That's not too much to ask, is it?

Reference point #2: Memories of doing without

I know a man who has always been thankful for his shoes. When I asked him why, he replied, "When I was a boy during the Depression, my parents couldn't afford to buy new shoes for me. I put cardboard in my shoe bottoms whenever they got holes. When I walked through rain and snow, I had to keep replacing the cardboard. I've always been thankful for shoes because I've never forgotten wearing those shoes with holes in the soles."

His reference point for thankfulness was his childhood memory of worn-out shoes. If we think of the times when we did without, we'll become more thankful for what we have. That's why God told the children of Israel to remember how He brought them out of the house of slavery (see Deut. 8:14). He wanted that experience to be a reference point in their minds.

Stirring up your memory of a time when you lacked will create a reference point for thanking God for everything you have.

Reference point #3: Losing blessings and recovering them

Sometimes we don't realize the value of our blessings until we lose them, like my wife's lost diamond. My father had to undergo radiation treatments for throat cancer. The therapy damaged his taste buds so that he couldn't taste food. His inability to enjoy a meal made eating a dreaded duty. The doctors told him that his taste might return after the treatments were finished, but no one could say for certain.

Weeks passed, then months. Every meal became a forced feeding to keep him alive. After eating flavorless food for over a year, he sat down for dinner one evening. Reluctantly, he forced the fork inside his mouth and discovered that his taste had returned. What most people would call a bland dinner became the best meal he had eaten in his life.

Through losing his taste and then regaining it, my father learned to relish each morsel as never before. He became thankful for the ability to taste because he now had a reference point. He would never forget what it was like to eat tasteless food.

You don't have to lose something in order to be thankful. You can develop a "taste" for your blessings by simply realizing what life would be like without them.

Reference point #4: Comparison with a worse situation

A woman in our church had a seriously ill son. The initial diagnosis revealed that he had either mononucleosis or cancer. The entire church prayed for a good report. After the tests revealed he didn't have cancer, his mother was ecstatic. Although having mononucleosis wouldn't normally be called good news, it's wonderful news when compared to a life-threatening problem.

The mother found a reference point by comparing a bad situation with a worse scenario. The more reference points we have in our mind, the greater our ability to focus on our blessings and thank God for them.

You might think you already have the worst-case scenario. No one could possibly have a situation worse than yours. Remember, perspective is always in the eye of the beholder.

Clarence was a very poor man with a large family. It took every penny he had to take care of his six children. Three of the children had worn out their shoes and needed new ones, but the family also needed a washing machine. He had to make a choice which to buy, so he decided to look for a used washer. He saw an ad in the paper with an address of someone selling a used washing machine.

He went to the house, which was located in a very nice neighborhood. With some resentment and envy in his heart, he rang the doorbell. He wondered why some people had so much and he had so little. A man and wife came to the door, and Clarence asked how much they wanted for their washer. The couple offered to sell it to him for a very low price. Clarence told him he appreciated it, because he had to choose between buying a washing machine or shoes for three of his children. Then he added, "You folks really have it good. I'll bet you've never had to worry about buying shoes."

Without saying a word, the woman teared up and left the room. Clarence gulped. "I'm sorry, I didn't mean to say anything wrong."

The man explained, "That's OK. The problem is we only have one child, a little girl, and she's never walked a step in her life. She's confined to a wheelchair. She's never been able to wear out a pair of shoes."

Clarence went home that day with an old washing machine, but with a new perspective. He asked God to forgive him of his envy and thanked God for those three pairs of worn-out shoes—and his children's ability to wear them out.[2]

Reference point #5: Experiences that haven't happened to us

Dale Carnegie once went through a prolonged period of depression. To pull out of his despair, he wrote a list of everything important to him. He then imagined what life would be like without his blessings. He listed a number of hypothetical tragedies:

- My children are in jail.
- My wife has left me.
- I'm flat broke.
- My health is ruined.

After completing his list, Carnegie drew a line through each misfortune that wasn't true. He crossed off the entire list. His reference points for thankfulness were all those bad experiences that never came to pass. His depression soon lifted.[3]

What calamities have you escaped? Thank God for the bad things that *haven't* happened to you.

～ Thanks, but No Thanks

Have you ever heard of counterfeit thankfulness? It's saying thankful words but from an ungrateful heart. I call it "Thanks, but no thanks." Jesus rebuked the Pharisees by saying, "This people honors Me with their lips, but their heart is far away from Me" (Matt. 15:8).

We can easily deceive ourselves into thinking that we have a thankful heart simply because we say grateful words. Phony thankfulness gives lip service out of obligation or courtesy. If someone opens the door, we may say thank you, but we aren't really thankful. We're just being polite. We might automatically say thank you when we receive a gift out of habit, or because we have good manners.

To combat counterfeit thankfulness, Paul wrote, "Let the word of Christ richly dwell within you . . . singing with thankfulness in your hearts to God" (Col. 3:16). True thankfulness resides only inside an appreciative heart.

Thankfulness is a powerful tool for correcting perspective. It has incredible authority, with the ability to drive discontentment, pessimism, worry, and discouragement out of our hearts. Once those glasses are removed, our perspective will *greatly* improve.

I believe many people become depressed because they fail to give thanks on a daily basis. They focus on dark clouds and never see the silver linings. Rather than being grateful for all things, they don't try to find even one thing to be thankful for.

Novelist A. J. Cronin tells of a physician friend who often prescribed a "thank you" cure for depressed patients. For a period of six weeks, the patients had to say "thank you" for everything they received and to record each incident. The doctor said he had a remarkable cure rate because his depressed patients simply learned to look for something good and give thanks for it.[4]

Many depressed people can actually *thank* their way out of depression. Not a token "thank you" every now and then, but a radical change in perspective that's constantly on the lookout for God's blessings and giving thanks with a grateful heart. Try it and you'll see. Continual thankfulness will open your eyes to a world full of blessings and will drive depression away.

> Many depressed people can actually *thank* their way out of depression.

⌒ Cultivating a Thankful Heart

Three aspects are necessary for cultivating a thankful heart. We need to be immediately, continually, and unconditionally thankful.

1. Immediately Thankful

God wants us to start thanking Him the moment He blesses us. When Jesus healed the leper, the first thing He ordered the healed man to do was show himself to the priest and make an offering (see Luke 5:14). Jesus wanted him to express his thankfulness by promptly presenting a gift. If we don't learn to respond quickly with an act of gratitude, we'll probably forget to thank God.

Thanksgiving is "thanks" with "giving." "He who offers a sacrifice of thanksgiving honors Me" (Ps. 50:23). Express your thankfulness sacrificially—either through words, gifts, or actions. True gratefulness always finds a way to express appreciation to God in a tangible way.

2. Continually Thankful

Ephesians 5:20 says, "Always giving thanks for all things in the name of our Lord Jesus Christ to God." Thankfulness is not only an attitude; it's also a discipline. "Always giving thanks" means to be *continually* thankful throughout each day. God has given us far more blessings than we've ever thanked Him for. Don't just give thanks a couple of times a day but several times every hour.

The moment you wake up in the morning, thank God for another day of life. Thank Him for saving you forever. Give thanks as you brush your teeth, remembering that many people in the world don't have toothpaste. While you drive your car, thank Him for your transportation. Throughout the day, notice all the blessings you have, and give thanks. By the end of the day, you should have thanked God at least fifty times.

> God has given us far more blessings than we've ever thanked Him for.

Little Jenny sat down to eat dinner with her family. She looked at the leftovers and said, "Hey, wait a minute. We thanked God for this *last* night!"

Just because we've thanked God once for something doesn't mean we can't thank Him again. God loves to hear His children expressing gratitude from thankful hearts. I've thanked God hundreds, perhaps thousands, of times for the same blessings.

Rather than giving thanks one time for a meal before you eat, why not try thanking Him throughout the entire meal as you eat it? Be sure to thank Him immediately, but also thank Him continually.

3. Unconditionally Thankful

God's will begins with a grateful heart. "In everything give thanks; for this is God's will for you in Christ Jesus" (1 Thess. 5:18). Why does God say to give thanks in everything? Maybe it's because He wants His children always to have thankful hearts regardless of circumstances.

If you think your conditions must improve before you can thank God, just remember that Jonah thanked God from inside a whale! (Jon. 2:9). "Always giving thanks for all things" means we should be unconditionally thankful at all times. Although God knows bad things happen to everyone, He wants us to maintain a grateful heart during difficult times. An unconditionally thankful heart is crucial to keeping a healthy perspective.

Most people have a short list of things they're thankful for and an extremely long complaint list. Both good and bad are intermingled in every circumstance. Unconditional thankfulness is developed by deliberately focusing on the best in any given situation.

Prices Just Went Up

Has it ever occurred to you that the things you now have were once things you were trying to get? Yet you soon forgot how badly you wanted them. It doesn't take long to start losing appreciation.

A friend of mine bought a brand-new $125 ski bib for a nickel at a garage sale. At one time, the original owner wanted it badly enough to pay $125. As time passed, the owner's appreciation for the item dwindled down to a mere five cents. Many people put garage sale prices on their blessings, ready to surrender them to the lowest bidder. Are you one of those people?

A magazine publisher asked a number of prominent people from all over the world what would make them happier. An architect said he wanted a garden and a greenhouse. A noted author said, "Give me perfect health, and I'll be happy." A well-known politician wished for a Vermont farm with apple orchard. However, one particular man gave an especially insightful answer. He said, "I would like to be given an even greater ability to appreciate all that I now have."[5]

> Has it ever occurred to you that the things you now have were once things you were trying to get?

You will gain a new appreciation for your blessings by simply raising the value of everything you own. God's blessings are worth a lot more than you realize. Just change the price tags to reflect their true worth.

Remove those garage sale stickers. Quadruple the prices.

Start focusing on your blessings, and it won't be long before you discover a lost diamond—the jewel of appreciation.

SEVENTEEN

Maintaining Your Perspective

Discipline is anything that causes what is believed in the heart to have demonstrable consequences in our daily life.

~ EUGENE PETERSON

I'VE BEEN thinking about taking an aerobics class to get back into shape. Only one problem. The YMCA class starts at 5:30 a.m. I've thought long and hard about committing to an exercise program that starts so early in the morning. I've decided to take the plunge. I know that if I don't make a commitment, I won't follow through. I'm recording my experiences as I write this chapter.

WEEK 1: When we began the workout, I found myself awkwardly following the instructor's movements. She's a petite young lady who can twist her body into various pretzel positions.

"One, two, three, four, and again. . . . Now take your leg and put it way up here, grab your other leg, and . . ."

At the end of the workout, we had a cooldown routine. We laid on our sides, stretching for a few moments, which was my favorite exercise of the day. I came home feeling nauseated. Getting into shape is going to be harder than I realized, but I'm determined to go through with it.

WEEK 2: It's only the second week, and the instructor has already added some new exercises. Just when I was getting the old routines down, she's making us do more funny movements. It's somewhat embarrassing as I watch myself in the mirror, stumbling a movement or two behind everyone else. I don't feel quite as nauseated as I did last week. I've lost a couple of pounds.

WEEK 3: It wasn't quite as hard to get out of bed today as it was on the first day. My instructor changed the exercises again. I think she's trying to find every unused muscle in my body so that she can make them sore. I wonder if she realizes that I'm writing about her. I've now lost four pounds. I'm realizing that toning my body is a gradual process, not something that happens overnight.

Over a year has passed since I took that class and wrote the above words. We moved to another state, but I've lost fifteen pounds by jogging, lifting weights, and modifying my diet. I changed my body by consistently following through with my decision.

Reshaping your perspective demands the same discipline as reshaping your body. Your outlook won't change overnight. It may take weeks or even months to correct the perception problem. A healthy perspective can be maintained only by renewing your mind daily. Unhealthy thoughts must go. Godly thoughts must take their place.

Every morning when you climb out of bed you choose how to view your world. Discipline yourself at the beginning of each day to look upward. Thank God throughout the day for everything you have. See God in ultimate control of everything that happens. When Satan makes a move, watch for God's countermoves. Seeing life from God's perspective requires a continual revision of your outlook.

> Reshaping your perspective demands the same discipline as reshaping your body.

View every day as a special occasion. Savor each moment. Seek to find the best in every circumstance. Realize that your time on earth is a privilege, not a right. And don't forget to take inventory.

Taking Inventory

Author David McLennon worked at his first job in a small-town general store when he was thirteen years old. This was back in the days before malls and supermarket chains. He would sweep the floor, bag items for customers, and stock shelves. One Saturday he heard the store owner say to one of the clerks, "It's that time of the year again—time to take inventory."

McLennon said that he had never heard the word "inventory" before and didn't know what it meant. He asked the owner, "Sir, what's an inventory?"

The owner explained, "It's a time when you make a list of everything you have. You count every item in the store from groceries on the shelves to wrapping paper and string."

"Why do you take inventory?"

"Well, it's easy to forget exactly how much we have," the owner replied. "So every now and then we have to take an inventory just to see everything that we have."[1]

How often do you take inventory? Are you aware of the many blessings you now possess?

~ Your "Awarehouse"

Try this exercise: Each time your hand touches an object in your house, think what it would be like to be *without* it, and then thank God for it. You'll be stunned by what you discover—just in your own bathroom.

Doorknob. Light switch. Shower curtain. Shower knob. Water. Soap. Shampoo. Conditioner. Towel. Towel bar. Razor. Shaving cream. Toilet. Toilet paper. Makeup (include all items). Toothbrush. Toothpaste. Deodorant. Floss. Mouthwash. Hairbrush. Hair spray.

Do you realize that if you were born in a Third World country, you might not own any of these things? If you can't thank God for an item, perhaps you don't need it. Give it to someone who can use it.

Taking inventory requires you to search and find every blessing in your life and give thanks to God. Perhaps this is what Paul meant when he said, "Always giving thanks for all *things* in the name of our Lord Jesus Christ to God, even the Father" (Eph. 5:20). Each blessing you take notice of counts as one item in your "awarehouse." Perspective is maintained by becoming aware of each good thing you have.

Listed below are some commonly ignored blessings that I thank God for daily. Although not everything in my inventory may apply to you, you can create your own list. Do *not* write down your blessings on paper, because reading your list to God every day could quickly become impersonal. The privilege of thanking God might turn into a legalistic job instead of a liberating joy. Your awarehouse items must be found through seeing them with your heart.

- *Salvation.* If Jesus has saved you for all eternity, how can you not thank Him every day? I thank Him for dying for my sins, giving me eternal life, and changing my destiny. This is usually the first thing I thank Him for each morning.

- *Another day of life.* Thank Him for the privilege of living another day on earth. Ask Him to show you how to make today count for eternity. This is the first day of the rest of your life. It could also be the last day of the rest of your life.
- *Family.* If you're married, thank Him for your spouse. Thank Him for your children, and pray for God to bless your family. If you're single, thank Him for the freedom of your singleness. Thank Him for your parents.
- *Friends.* If you don't have any friends, whose fault is that? Go out and make some.
- *Health.* If you're sick, ask the Lord to heal you. If you're healthy, have you ever thanked God that all the organs in your body are functioning properly?
- *The roof over your head.* Count yourselves blessed to have shelter. What if you had to live outside in the cold or rain, like many people in other countries?
- *Air-conditioning and heating.* Turn a dial and the room temperature changes to make you comfortable. Many people in the world perspire all night long in bed because they don't have cooling. Have you *ever* thanked God for these comforts?
- *Hot and cold running water.* People in Third World countries don't have plumbing in their homes, much less heated water for showers and baths. Do you thank God every time you take a shower or bath? I do.
- *Toilets.* What an incredible privilege to have indoor toilets! Until recently, most of the people since the creation of the earth never had this blessing. On cold, wintry evenings they had to go outside to an outhouse. Remember this the next time you go to the bathroom in the middle of the night. And thank God for your toilet.

- *Clean water.* Many people in the world drink dirty, contaminated water, filled with parasites and other organisms. Do you thank God for clean water?
- *Closets filled with clothes.* While much of the world yearns for clothing to keep warm, you have more than you need and choose clothes based upon the latest fashion. No need to feel guilty, but you have an incredible need to thank God and share with others.
- *Electricity.* Never take this luxury for granted. You usually don't have to bother with lighting lanterns and candles. This power source operates all your modern conveniences. Do you continually thank God for this blessing? I do.
- *Medicine.* Thank God for the medical remedies to keep you in good health, rather than complaining about their cost. At least medicine is available to you.
- *Refrigerators, ovens, stoves, Crock-Pots, microwaves.* You have the most modern ways to preserve and prepare your food. You don't have to chop wood every day so you can cook over an open fire. Thank the Lord for these things.
- *Fresh and prepared foods.* When you go to the grocery store, you can select from nearly every kind of food imaginable. You don't have to grow your own groceries. Where you live probably doesn't grow bananas, pineapples, or mangoes. These fruits are brought to you from great distances away and from foreign countries for your convenience. Thank the Lord for fresh fruit, vegetables, fish, beef, and even live lobsters. Go to the frozen food section and choose food that's already prepared for you. You have more blessings at your fingertips than most kings had who have lived throughout the history of the world. I think about this

every time that I'm in a grocery store and thank God for His provision.

- *Restaurants.* What kind of food would you like to eat? Chinese, Mexican, Italian, or American? Fast food or romantic dinner? Just take your pick where you want to eat. Do you appreciate this blessing, or do you complain about the slow service?
- *Cars.* Most people in the world don't have their own automobiles. As you travel in your car every day, thank Him for that luxury. Thank Him for the availability of gasoline no matter what the price per gallon is.
- *Music.* Do you thank God for music? For Christian music? As you travel in your car, you have the finest musicians in the world playing on your radio, tape, or compact disc player. If you don't like a particular song, press a button and you can hear a different one. Have you thanked God for this luxury?
- *Bibles and Christian books.* You probably own several copies of God's Word. I hope you read them. And today, there are more Christian books than ever—bringing you information from godly teachers to help you in every area of your Christian walk.
- *Churches.* Thank God for the Body of Christ. If you aren't being spiritually fed in your current church, find one that preaches the Bible and get involved there. Thank Him for the privilege of serving in His body.
- *Your job.* God gives you the power to get wealth (see Deut. 8:18). He's the one who provided your job, so thank Him for it rather than complaining about your work conditions.

If you will thank God for each item in your awarehouse every day, I promise you that your perspective will improve significantly. You'll learn to see blessings, even in your darkest hour.

On August 14, 2003, the power grid in the Northeast failed, causing the largest blackout in United States history. Suddenly, fifty million residents from New York to Michigan found themselves without electricity for the afternoon and evening. Elevators stopped. Traffic lights went out. Planes were grounded. Tens of thousands of people jammed the streets of New York City, all desperately trying to walk home before the night fell. Many New Yorkers slept on the streets that night.

The next morning with the electricity still off, a television reporter interviewed several people on a New York City street. The reporter rushed over to a lady who wore a big smile on her face and said, "You are the only one smiling around here. Why?"

The woman said, "I'm thankful for the little things—like toilet paper and water."

The reporter, grasping the insight of the comment, replied, "Hmm, it's perspective, isn't it?"

Yes, it is. It's all about perspective.

And now you know the secret about how to change your perspective. All that's left is to put what you've learned into practice each day.

I pray you'll do it.

Notes

Part 1

1. As reported on NBC's "Today Show," July 25, 1996.

Chapter 2

1. Bennett Daviss, "A Mind of Its Own," *Ambassador Magazine* (TransWorld Airlines), February 1999, 22–26.
2. Ibid.
3. Ibid.
4. Jan Barclay, *Living and Enjoying the Fruit of the Spirit* (Chicago: Moody Press, 1976), 55.

Chapter 3

1. The author has written several successful books since that time and is doing well.

Chapter 4

1. King Duncan, *Amusing Grace* (Knoxville: Seven Worlds Corporation, 1993), 269.

Chapter 5

1. *Our Daily Bread,* Grand Rapids: RBC Ministries, July 27, 1994.
2. Sally E. Stuart, *Christian Writers' Market Guide* (Colorado Springs: WaterBrook Press, 2001), 194.
3. Kent Crockett, *The 911 Handbook* (Peabody, Mass.: Hendrickson Publishers, 1997).

Chapter 6

1. *Preaching,* May-June 1997, 58.
2. Compiled by Ted Kyle and John Todd, *A Treasury of Bible Illustrations* (Chattanooga, Tenn.: AMG Publishers, 1995), 165.
3. Ed Diener, *The Futurist* (University of Illinois at Urbana-Champaign, Office of Public Affairs, News Bureau, 1201 Nevada Street, Urbana, Ill.), November-December 1993, 7.
4. Ibid.
5. BBC News, February 12, 2001.

Chapter 7

1. Charles Swindoll, *The Tale of the Tardy Oxcart* (Nashville: Word Publishing, 1998), 311.
2. Paul Tan, comp., *Encyclopedia of 7700 Illustrations* (Rockville, Md.: Assurance Publishers, 1979), 646.
3. Ralph Earle, *Word Meanings in the New Testament* (Peabody, Mass.: Hendrickson Publishers, 1997), 239.

Chapter 8

1. Leanne Payne, *Restoring the Christian Soul Through Healing Prayer* (Wheaton, Ill.: Crossway Books, 1991), 32.
2. Louis Harris, *Inside America* (New York: Vintage Books, 1987).
3. Tim LaHaye, *How to Win Over Depression* (Grand Rapids: Zondervan Publishing House, 1974), 141.
4. Raymond McHenry, *The Best of In Other Words*, 1996, 22, 23.

Chapter 10

1. "Man bitten by snake uses skin as tourniquet," Associated Press, May 11, 1996.
2. Warren Wiersbe, *Be Wise* (Wheaton, Ill.: Victor Books, 1984), 132.
3. From *The Reconciler*, the newsletter of the Christian Conciliation Service of Kansas City, March 1991.

Chapter 11

1. Kent Crockett, *The 911 Handbook* (Peabody, Mass.: Hendrickson Publishers, 1997), 97, 98.

Chapter 12

1. Haddon W. Robinson, *What Jesus Said* (Grand Rapids: Discovery House, 1991).
2. Tan, *Encyclopedia of 7700 Illustrations*, 1445.
3. Ernest Kurtz and Katherine Ketcham, *The Spirituality of Imperfection: Storytelling and the Journey to Wholeness* (New York: Bantam Books, 1992).

Chapter 13

1. "Violent film inspired teens, police say," *Detroit News*, March 25, 1994.
2. "Movie may have influenced teen to kill," United Press International, March 7, 1995.
3. "Cruise ships on lookout for 'Titanic' copycats," Associated Press, June 24, 1998.

Chapter 14

1. *Our Daily Bread*, May 17, 1989.
2. Helen and Larry Eisenberg, *The Public Speakers Handbook of Humor* (Grand Rapids, Mich.: Baker Book House, 1967), 227.

Chapter 15

1. *Reader's Digest*, May 1999, 126.
2. Ron Lee Davis, *Courage to Begin Again* (Eugene, Oreg.: Harvest House, 1988).

Chapter 16

1. *Hope Health Letter*, cited in *Leadership*, winter 1996, 74 (this was a sermon illustration and no other information is available).
2. Brian Harbour, *Brian's Lines*, Vol. 6, No. 3, March 1990, 13.
3. Norman Vincent Peale, "Being Thankful Makes Everything Better" (Pawling, N.Y.: Foundation for Christian Living, 1961), 7–84.
4. *Dynamic Preaching* (Knoxville, Tenn.: Seven Worlds Corporation, July 1995).
5. Luther J. Thompson, *Through Discipline to Joy* (Nashville: Broadman Press, 1966), 44.

Chapter 17

1. www.esermons.com November 2001.

Study Guide

CHAPTER 1 In the Eye of the Beholder

Read the story about one woman's reaction to Pastor Ed Manning. Ask the members in your study group to share a time when they wrongly perceived a situation.

Discuss how mismatched perspectives can create problems in relationships. (Examples: husband/wife, parent/child, boss/employee.)

Why does Satan try to distort our perspectives?

Read the story about the three people wearing pink, yellow, and blue sunglasses viewing the white paper. Discuss how different perspectives can cause disagreement.

Discuss three ways that our perspective affects us.

We can see faults in others but are blind to our own. If *you* were married to *you*, what attitudes in your spouse would upset you?

If everyone in the world all had identical perspectives, why would we still have conflict?

Read Proverbs 16:2. Discuss how God sees us differently than we see ourselves.

CHAPTER 2   The Heart of the Problem

Read Matthew 15:9. What are some of the attitudes and actions that come from our hearts? How do these attitudes mold a person's perspective?

Read the "Candid Camera" story. If you were copying your friend's video, what comments would be recorded on the tape? How does this relate to Luke 12:3?

Why does Proverbs 4:23 tell us to guard our hearts?

Discuss how our eyes and heart work together to form perspective (Matt. 5:28).

Why does God want to put a new heart and spirit within us? (Ezek. 36:26, 27)

When you accept Christ into your life, He calls you out of darkness into light (1 Pet. 2:9). Why do people squint when they leave a dark room and enter a bright room? How does this apply to perspective?

Read Mark 8:23–25. Why do you suppose Jesus performed this healing in stages?

CHAPTER 3   Discontentment Glasses

Discuss the story about Phil wanting to change jobs. What can we learn from his experience?

Discontentment creates an imaginary world. Why do we tend to see others as living in a problem-free world?

Jonah ran away from his divine assignment. Why does discontentment compel us to run from God's will?

Read Philippians 4:11, 12. What are the two "schools" of learning and why do we need to learn from both?

Where is the only place we will find the greenest grass? (Ps. 23:1, 2) Why?

How do you think Paul learned to be happy in prison? What did he accomplish in prison that impacts our lives today?

What does it mean to "play the cards that have been dealt to you"?

CHAPTER 4   Pessimist Glasses

How is perspective like having a cameraman inside your heart?

Discuss the story of the hot dog salesman. How can a pessimistic attitude create a depressing world to live in?

Using the example of the dot on the piece of paper, explain how a closed-in viewpoint leaves God out of the picture.

Do you think that Karl Wallenda's negative focus contributed to his accident? How does pessimism affect our confidence?

How is complaining a sign of pessimism?

Read Philippians 4:8. List the different kinds of thoughts that should saturate our minds.

Kent exchanged his joy for $7. Name some circumstances that can steal your joy.

Read 1 Thessalonians 5:18. What is God's will for you in this verse?

How is Roy Parrino able to find treasure in a sewer? How does this principle apply to perspective?

CHAPTER 5 **Rejection Glasses**

Discuss this statement: "Rejection isn't what happens to us, but *how we interpret* what happens to us."

If you invite rejection into your heart, how will you feel?

Why didn't anyone greet the pastor's friend after the church service? Explain why some people cause their own rejection.

Discuss the story about the woman wearing the nice dress. Explain how her warped perspective turned a compliment into an insult.

Read Romans 14:3. Why is it important to accept God's acceptance of us?

Read Matthew 10:14. Why did Jesus tell His disciples to shake the dust off their feet?

Read Romans 12:18. Why should you attempt to make peace with those who reject you? Explain how George Sullivan's attempt to make peace with his father changed his life.

CHAPTER 6 **Envy Glasses**

Envy compares positions, possessions, and property with others. Discuss the different kinds of envy (salary, mansion, talent).

What does it mean to "covet"?

Read Exodus 20:17. Referring to the story of Robbie's hamburger, discuss how Kent learned how *not* to covet in his head but how *to* covet in his heart.

What did the all-day workers do when the one-hour workers were paid the same amount? (Matt. 20:11). How are modern-day laborers guilty of the same thing?

Read James 4:1, 2. What was the source of their quarrels and conflicts? Why?

Discuss this statement: "Love your neighbor, not what your neighbor has."

How can seeing God as your provider help remove your envy glasses?

Explain what "being content with your wages" means and doesn't mean.

CHAPTER 7   Jealousy Glasses

Discuss some differences between envy and jealousy.

What is jealousy rooted in? How does mistrust create jealousy?

Discuss this statement: "You cannot make anyone love you." What is the lesson we can learn from the kitchen cupboard?

What can we learn about assuming from the Sam Pritchard story?

Read Matthew 22:37. How does jealousy violate the greatest commandment?

Read 1 Corinthians 13:4, 5. Discuss how God's love, *agape*, acts and reacts.

According to Psalm 84:11, what does God promise to those who walk uprightly?

CHAPTER 8   Inferiority Glasses

The word *hate* doesn't always mean to "cease loving." What does it mean in Luke 14:26?

According to author Leanne Payne, why is it dangerous to hate the soul that God loves?

Read Numbers 13:32, 33. Discuss this statement: "The way we see ourself determines how we believe others see us."

Define "self-image." How can a warped self-image be compared to the crazy house of mirrors at the carnival?

Read 2 Timothy 3:1, 2. What does it mean to be a "lover of self" in this passage? Distinguish between "self" as personhood and "selfishness" as an attitude.

Read Romans 9:20. What does this teach us about accepting ourselves as God's creation? How did King David view himself? (Ps. 139:14).

Why was the woman set free when Dr. Michaelson quoted Psalm 100:3?

What does it mean to love your neighbor as yourself? (Matt. 22:39).

CHAPTER 9   Wounded Glasses

Discuss the insight that Kent received when he placed his hand on the man's wounded shoulder.

Why are wounded people easily injured by innocent comments?

Discuss the story of the dog named "Spot." Why did Spot view the boy who wanted to play "fetch" with suspicion?

Discuss this statement: "A person with a toothache has a hard time loving others." Why?

What is a "victim mentality"?

Read John 5:1–9. Why did Jesus ask him, "Do you wish to get well?"

Read James 5:16. What does confession have to do with healing?

Discuss the story about Laura. Why wasn't twenty years enough time to heal her? What was the key to her being healed?

CHAPTER 10 Bitterness Glasses

What did Paul do when the snake bit him? (Acts 28:5). If you don't shake off the serpent, what will it continue to do?

What is the first stage in the bitterness process? What must you do during this stage?

Explain why you get angry. What does Ephesians 4:26 instruct you to do?

What is unforgivingness and what does it do to our hearts? Why don't we like to think of our unforgivingness as hate?

Define "bitterness."

Read Matthew 5:38, 39. Why does Jesus instruct us to not resist an evil person?

Why are bitter people filled with deadly poison?

Discuss how monkeys are captured. What can we learn from them about letting go?

What can we learn from Stephen about being an "instant for-giver"? (Acts 7:60).

Read Micah 6:8. How does forgiveness relate to mercy?

CHAPTER 11   Judgmental Glasses

What is the difference between judging and criticism?

What do the biblical terms "bless" and "curse" mean?

According to James 3:9–11, why is it wrong to bless the Creator and then curse His creation?

What have judgmental people lost?

When you drive down a highway, why do you notice the vehicles that look exactly like your own? How does this relate to people who judge others? (Rom. 2:1, 3).

Explain why the man with the dirty windshield blamed the station attendant.

Give some examples of people who make judgments based on incomplete information.

What two things are required to take the log out of our own eye? (Matt. 7:5).

As your perspective adjusts, what will also change? (Matt. 12:34).

As your compassion increases what will decrease?

CHAPTER 12   Lust Glasses

Discuss Peter Lord's statement: "Temptation is trying to fulfill a legitimate, God-given desire in an illegitimate way."

To break free from sexual addiction, what must a person become desperate for?

Read Matthew 22:37. How can you love God with your mind?

What is the only way to overcome lust? (Gal. 5:16). What is your only source of holiness?

Why do some people have more temptations than others?

Read Ephesians 4:27. What does it mean to not give the devil an opportunity?

Fasting means to go without food while praying. What does fasting do to your drives?

Discuss the story of the boy shopping for the cookie jar. How will an accountability partner help you?

CHAPTER 13 Worry Glasses

Read the three examples at the beginning of the chapter. What did they all do alike after watching the movies?

Read the story of the package delivery driver's wife. Discuss the statement: "You act, not necessarily upon what is true, but on what you *believe* to be true."

Why does Satan create an unreal world through your imaginations?

What is the difference between a prayer *worrier* and a prayer *warrior*?

What does it mean to "cast down" an imagination? (2 Cor. 5:10).

How do we "take every thought captive"? (2 Cor. 5:10).

What must scuba divers do when they think their air bubbles are going sideways? How does this relate to Proverbs 3:5?

CHAPTER 14 Discouragement Glasses

What did David do when he was at the lowest point in his life? (1 Sam. 30:4, 6). How can we tap into a power that is outside of ourselves?

What did the apostle Paul discover when he was weak? (2 Cor. 12:9).

What lessons can be learned from the story of the king who placed the boulder in the road?

Why does Hebrews 10:35, 36 tell us to not throw away our confidence?

What are many of God's blessings waiting behind? (Matt. 7:7).

What truth is demonstrated in the experiment of the iron ball and cork? How does this apply to faith?

What does it mean that "God has the last word"? (Rom. 8:28).

CHAPTER 15 Seeing as God Sees

Read John 19:10, 11. When Jesus stood before Pilate, how did they each view the situation differently?

Discuss how Joseph saw God in control in spite of his circumstances (Gen. 45:5–8).

What does God's "sovereignty" mean? (See Genesis 50:20).

Read Romans 8:35–37. What does it mean that we "overwhelmingly conquer"?

How was Jesus moved when He saw people? (Matt. 9:36).

What can we learn about value through the story of the crumpled $20 bill?

Discuss the different points under "Exercising Your Perspective."

CHAPTER 16 Focusing on Blessings

What lesson did Kent and Cindy learn about thankfulness from their incident with the lost diamond?

Read Deuteronomy 8:10–14. What causes us to forget the Lord?

How did the wise man create a "reference point" for the man living in the tiny hut?

Discuss how "theoretically trading places" with people in other parts of the world can change our perspective.

Why was the man who put cardboard in his soles always thankful for his shoes? Why is it important to stir up a memory of a time when you lacked?

What was Kent's father's new reference point after he recovered his ability to taste food?

What is "counterfeit thankfulness"? (Matt. 15:8).

Discuss the three elements in cultivating a thankful heart.

Why did the person at the garage sale sell a $125 ski bib for a nickel? What does this tell us about appreciation?

CHAPTER 17 Maintaining Your Perspective

Discuss why reshaping your perspective demands the same discipline as reshaping your body.

What does it mean to "take inventory"? How can we apply this to the many blessings we possess?

Carefully discuss each item in the "awarehouse" list.

More Information on Dennis "The Swan" Swanberg

Videos/Audios/CDs

Loosen Up, Laugh, and Live
Back to Back with Laughter
Is Your Love Tank Full?
Laughter from the Rafters
Smiling with the Saints
Christmas with the Swan
Planting Shade Trees
Life on the Lighter Side
Baseball, Buffets, and a Barrel of Laughs

Books

Is Your Love Tank Full, or Are You Loving on Empty?
Swan's Soup and Salad
Why ADHD Doesn't Mean Disaster

TV Shows

The Dennis Swanberg Show on TBN
Swan's Place on FamNet

Product/Ministry Information:

Swanberg Christian Ministries
P. O. Box 1495
West Monroe, Louisiana 71294
(318) 325-9044 (office)
(318) 325-0012 (fax)
www.dennisswanberg.com